TEACHING
AMERICAN
HISTORY
THROUGH THE NOVEL

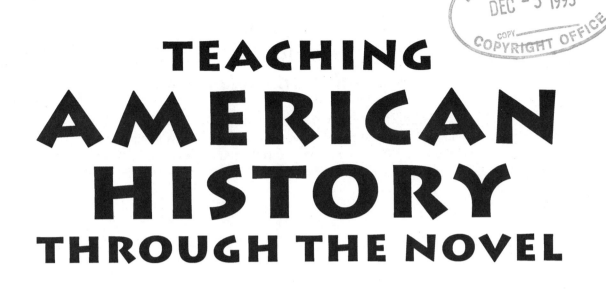

W9-ABY-706

SHARON BANNISTER WITH TWYLA R. WELLS

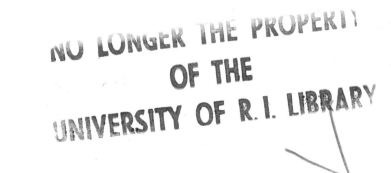

J. WESTON
WALCH
PUBLISHER
PORTLAND, MAINE

User's Guide
to
Walch Reproducible Books

As part of our general effort to provide educational materials which are as practical and economical as possible, we have designated this publication a "reproducible book." The designation means that purchase of the book includes purchase of the right to limited reproduction of all pages on which this symbol appears:

Here is the basic Walch policy: We grant to individual purchasers of this book the right to make sufficient copies of reproducible pages for use by all students of a single teacher. This permission is limited to a single teacher, and does not apply to entire schools or school systems, so institutions purchasing the book should pass the permission on to a single teacher. Copying of the book or its parts for resale is prohibited.

Any questions regarding this policy or requests to purchase further reproduction rights should be addressed to:

Permissions Editor
J. Weston Walch, Publisher
321 Valley Street • P. O. Box 658
Portland, Maine 04104-0658

—J. Weston Walch, Publisher

1 2 3 4 5 6 7 8 9 10
ISBN 0-8251-2746-7

Contents

ACKNOWLEDGMENTS

Libraries used during the preparation of this book include the Bowling Green State University Jerome Library (Bowling Green, Ohio); the Findlay-Hancock County Public Library (Findlay, Ohio); the Lima Public Library (Lima, Ohio); the Mary Louise Childs Collection of the University of Findlay Shafer Library (Findlay, Ohio); the Michigan State University Library (East Lansing, Michigan); and the Wood County Public Library (Bowling Green, Ohio).

During my work on the book, my mother and my eldest brother died. Both were aware of my research. This book is dedicated to the memory of my mother, Ruth Virginia; my brother, Kerry; and my father, Robert Merrill Bannister.

As this project developed, I engaged a research assistant, Twyla R. Wells. Over time, her work went beyond the nature of research assistant and reflected such quality that I asked her to be my associate author. Without her dedication and support, the work would not have been finished. We both wish to thank friends and colleagues for their support.

INTRODUCTION

A novelist if he [or she] chooses, has a greater opportunity for faithful presentation of a bygone time than an historian, for the historian is compelled to a presentation of cause and effect and feels, as a rule, that he [or she] must present them through the lives and characters of 'famous' or 'historical' figures. My concern, however, has been with life as it was. . . .

—Walter D. Edmonds
in the Introduction to *Drums Along the Mohawk*

It is the business of the novel to picture the daily life in the most exact terms possible, with an absolute and clear sense of proportion.

—William Dean Howells to Stephen Crane
in the Introduction to *The Rise of Silas Lapham*

The Alliance Between History and Literature

This is a reproducible manual containing annotations of novels for use by middle-school, junior-high, and senior-high-school teachers of American history. The book contains over 300 annotations arranged in ways that allow teachers and students to use them in teaching and studying history. This manual can also be used—in whole or in part—by students working on their own, for one of its major purposes is to interest students in reading about history as an enjoyable activity.

The two quotations that begin the Introduction represent views on the relationship between the novel and its use in teaching history. Some of the strongest impressions and best memories I have of history in my undergraduate student days come from reading assigned novels in my history courses. The main part of my doctoral dissertation concentrated on an analysis of nineteenth-century English novels written by women. Since becoming a college and university professor, I have used novels as supplementary reading in English history, modern European history, and Russian history courses. I have team-taught with colleagues in courses that use novels as a focus. In one instance, I organized an entire English history course around novels. From this particular experience, I wrote *Teaching World History Through the Novel*, also a book of over 300 annotations of novels that could be used by junior-high and senior-high-school teachers in European history, world history, and world civilization courses. Students have often rated novels as the most valuable part of courses, or comment that they remember the novels most vividly. For many students, history "lives" in these novels. Teachers to whom I have spoken individually, in groups, or at conferences are continually intrigued by the use of novels in history courses and find that this technique gives them another tool in their collection of methods to teach history and make it relevant to students. My associate and I developed

Teaching American History Through the Novel as a logical extension of examining the relationship between the novel and history.

There are other advantages and characteristics of novels, however, that make them useful in teaching history. Literature in general often acts as a window looking into society, or as a mirror reflecting society. The novel is a particularly adaptable literary form and thus serves well as a vehicle to convey historical characteristics. It often provides an in-depth view of life at a given period. It deals with actual historical characters—or characters who could have existed during a particular historical period. The novel also describes actual historical circumstances—or circumstances that could have existed. Within its scope, the novel can include long historical periods to show evolution over time. Novelists often reflect, emphasize, or focus on the political, economic, social, and philosophical factors in a society. These factors are important in analyzing and interpreting trends, events, movements, and peoples.

In addition, students may identify more closely with characters in the lifelike situations created in novels than they do with typical textbook material. A revolution, a political assassination, the struggle to break out of a rigid class system, or the attempt to find meaning in life are usually much more apparent to students who read novels as part of their history coursework than to those who only know history as a list of names and events. Also, students can often make an intellectual leap from memorization of facts to working with historical information in a more creative way with the novel as a tool and an example. Novels can be the instrument by which students acquire or expand an interest in history.

Despite these advantages and characteristics of novels, there are many historians who do not support the use of novels as reading or as sources in history courses. There are many reasons advanced to support this opinion. Novels are not primary sources; they are not historical monographs, because they do not reflect standard historical research methods; they are imaginative works and do not always deal with an accepted body of historical facts or events; students will become confused with the blending of actual and imagined events and real and fictional persons. Thus, there is some distortion in the historical record if novels are accepted as a way to understand history.

All of these reasons for not using novels are understandable. However, I have always felt comfortable using novels in history courses as my personal experience reflects and as the advantages and characteristics of novels outlined above indicate. The historical record of written primary and secondary sources is incomplete. Individuals, institutions, and governments are selective as to what they leave or what is available for public perusal. Letters, diaries, memoirs, reminiscences, and autobiographies are often distorted depending on the goals of the writer, the capabilities of the writer, and when the records were written. Institutions and governments retain control over many aspects of records for periods of time or due to the nature of events. Many persons and events in history remain puzzles and mysteries because of incomplete records. It is always incumbent on the teacher to inform students about the problems of studying history. Fictionalizing history, as in docudramas or in novels, must also be carefully explained. However, with careful attention, teachers can create an appropriate historical background on which to play out the drama of the novel. My belief remains that there is likely to be as much historical accuracy and information in many novels as can be found in primary and secondary historical sources. The good historical novelist combines the talent of the literary artist with the research ability of the historian—a fact that historians and literary artists do not always fully appreciate.

My associate and I believe that American history provides an excellent storehouse of material for the novelist. Compared with much of the world, American history is short, focused on some enduring themes, and used as an example of emulation or rejection by many countries. The importance of America on the world scene has been apparent since the Civil War, and the dominance of American political, social, and economic institutions has been clear domestically and abroad since World War II. American novelists have selected from the unique American experience to forge an independent literary record apart from European roots since the early nineteenth century. Novelists have focused on searing, nation-forming events such as the American Revolution; destructive calamities such as the Civil War; the character-building, unique setting of the frontier and the West; the search for an American identity; America's character as displayed in various wars; the changing roles of women; and the continual, frustrating challenge of race relations. Novelists' reflections on these events have not only produced hundreds of novels since the early nineteenth century, but also include many examples of literary classics read all over the world.

HOW TO USE THIS BOOK

Teachers can use this book in a variety of ways. For some it will be a personal reference. For others it will be a resource for sharing with students. And for still others it will be a combination of both. All pages with a copyright notice at the bottom are designated by the publisher as reproducible. This means that most pages outside this teacher introduction may be copied in quantity sufficient to serve the students of a single teacher. One teacher might copy, cut apart, and pass out descriptions of books that seem appropriate to individual students. Another might place a small pile of the descriptions in a central location so that students can read through them and select their own novels. In small classes or for individual students, the entire book might be made available for browsing. Teachers will also find a wide range of ways to incorporate other reproducible materials from the book into their classes.

The manual as a whole reflects my belief in an interdisciplinary approach to teaching, or the combined use of history and literature. It is a source of organized information for the teacher who wishes to use fiction in American history courses. It serves as a reference guide to an alternate approach to teaching history, or as a reference guide for incorporating literature into existing teaching methods. Many middle-school, junior-high, and high-school teachers combine American history and American literature in cooperative or fully interdisciplinary team-taught ventures to present American civilization and culture in a more holistic view. Since American history is often taught at least twice to students in their careers (once in middle school and/or junior high and once in high school), careful planning can allow students to experience novels in one of these courses in a fully developed fashion. This manual can be a valuable source in planning such courses.

Over 300 novels are annotated in the book. All deal with material usually covered in a traditional two- or four-semester American history or American civilization course on the junior-high or senior-high level. In addition, dozens of the novels can be used in the middle-school setting, or from grades 5–6 to grades 8–9.

The Annotated Bibliography (Arrangement I)

Each of the annotations in this section contains the author, author dates, title, approximate number of pages, date of original publication, a description of the novel, and a coded indication of its reading and comprehension level. The annotations generally range from 100 to 200 words—long enough, we hope, to give teachers and students a good grasp of what it is in each novel. Each of the novels has been read and otherwise checked in at least one edition that is also the source of the approximate page counts. However, many titles are available in a number of editions that vary in length and design.

Teachers may find that particular editions they know and like are not available. In fact, they may not be able to find some out-of-print titles at all, for while all the titles are in some libraries, some are not in all libraries. In such cases, substitutions can often be found. If particular titles on the Civil War are not available, for example, then others will be. If a book on Native Americans capturing settlers in New England is not available, then a book on the same topic taking place in the Middle Atlantic states can be used instead. Teachers should note and take an interest in the inclusion of titles written from the 1840's to the 1990's. Historical novel writing has changed over the 150 years represented by titles in this book. For reviews of the most recent American historical novels, teachers can check such journals as *English Journal, School Library Journal,* or *Social Education.* Reviews must be read carefully and checked for accuracy by comparing them with the novels to be read. It is always wise to check with school librarians, college and university librarians, bookstores, book distributors or clearinghouses, or the varieties of books-in-print editions if teachers wish to order multiple copies for classroom use. Again, the number of pages may vary depending on the edition used and whether the book is in hardcover or paper-back. The descriptive paragraph places the novel in its historical time period and geographic setting, describes pertinent historical circumstances, and provides a brief summary of the plot.

The decisions on reading and comprehension levels were difficult to make. There are varieties of ways used by experts and teachers of reading to assess these. The number of words in a line, on a page, and number of pages in the book serve as three quantitative methods to arrive at reading and comprehension levels. The length and difficulty of words themselves, or the sophistication of the vocabulary, provides a way for teachers to judge levels. Teachers can obtain assistance with the quantitative and the vocabulary methods of assessment by consulting reading teachers in their schools or nearby colleges and universities. These persons have access to reading material on assessing reading and comprehension levels.

The characters in the book also give valuable clues to its difficulty. For example, most novels that use juveniles or adolescents—characters under the age of eighteen—as the main characters are considered novels for youngsters. Novels that include extensive illustrations are usually intended for younger readers. Generally, if the novel is classified in a library as *Juvenile* or *Adolescent,* the author has deliberately written the book for a younger audience. All of these traits—those reflecting the intent to attract young readers— usually mean the novels are easier to read.

All teachers generally have a good indication of the reading level of students in their classes. Even though many classes, including history, are grouped according to ability levels determined through testing, there is still a variety of reading levels present in every class. Some schools do not group their students according to aptitude, grades, or testing, so it is even more important that teachers know how well their students can read. The most common test (widely available and used nationwide) is the Nelson-Denny test, which assesses reading and comprehension by grade level. Teachers should seek assistance from reading instructors for information on this and other tests.

Taking the above into account, I have decided to use the basic designations of *easy, medium,* and *difficult.* These designations appear on the annotations as E, M, D, with read-ing level on the left and comprehension level on the right in this format: E/M. Teachers who do not wish to share this information with students can simply cover the codes before making student copies. The use of the designations is intended as a *general* guideline. Novels may vary somewhat within these categories.

The term *easy* indicates the following: In length, the novel is about 200 pages or less, is occasionally illustrated, sometimes has an introduction and/or end notes, and does not contain complex vocabulary. Events and persons are usually quite familiar or are major topics in American history. Almost all of these novels can be found in the public library in the juvenile or adolescent section intended for upper-grade-school, middle-school, and junior-high readers. For students at this level, for those who do not like to read, or for those with reading problems, the *easy* novels would probably be their first choice. These novels will also probably be easier to read for non-native English speakers and readers. Over a third (or over one hundred of the novels in the manual) are designated as *easy*.

Novels in the *medium* category are generally between 200 and 400 pages long. The contents usually include an introduction and/or explanatory notes. The vocabulary is more sophisticated. Merely because of its longer length, a *medium* novel is more difficult to read. The historical period, events, or movements may be complex, or may concern an unfamiliar topic not usually explored in great depth in a course. The persons who are the subjects may not be well known. For students who are at the correct reading level for their grade and/or those who have an interest in the topic, *medium* novels should pose no great problem. Students in grades 10–12 and excellent readers in grade 9 would be the primary audience for *medium* novels. Almost half of the novels in the manual are designated as *medium*.

A novel that is labeled *difficult* is generally over 400 pages long. An introduction and/or explanatory notes may often be included. The vocabulary is sophisticated. The topic of the novel centers on complex events that are dealt with in great detail. The novel also often focuses on some ethical or philosophical concern and/or deals with a little-known event or circumstance. For students who are very comfortably at or above grade level in reading, are very good students, and/or have a very strong interest in the topic, the *difficult* novels should be the choice. Students in grades 11 or 12 are the most likely to be able to read these novels. *Difficult* novels can also be used for excellent readers in lower grades, for college-preparatory classes or advanced placement classes, for individual students to take on as special projects, or for projects that might be done over a long vacation or in the summer. About one sixth of the novels in this book are labeled *difficult*.

Chronology, Themes, and Titles
(Arrangements II–IV)

The entries in this book are listed in *four ways*. The first and basic list is the annotated bibliography already described. It is arranged alphabetically by author, with titles given alphabetically under each author—except in the case of series, which are so noted and ordered by the logic of their content. This arrangement also serves as an author index.

The second list is *chronological*. The novels are grouped alphabetically, by author, into these major time periods: (I) A Land of Promise (pre-encounter–1600); (II) Building the Colonies (1600–1763); (III) Winning Independence (1763–1789); (IV) Building the

Nation (1789–1860); (V) The Nation Divides and Reunites (1850's–1870's); (VI) A Time of Transformation: Settlement and Closing of the Western Frontier (1860's–1917); (VII) A Time of Transformation: Industrialization, Urbanization, Modernization (1860's–1920's); (VIII) World War I and the 1920's; (IX) The Great Depression and the New Deal (1920's–1940's); (X) World War II at Home and Abroad (1939–1945); (XI) The Cold War and American Politics (1940's–1970's); (XII) The Civil Rights Era and America Today (1950's–1980's); (XIII) Possible Futures.

There are some novels that do not fit neatly into these categories. These have been placed in time periods in which a major part of the novel takes place, and they are noted by asterisk in the listings as crossing over time periods. Such novels are usually biographical novels or family sagas. Since teachers would probably prefer to use novels that concentrate on a particular event or narrow era, there are not too many novels crossing several time periods.

The third list is by *theme,* which is an approach particularly appropriate to American history. The novels are grouped alphabetically by author under each theme. Arrangement by theme allows teachers and students to use a selected group of novels over a longer period of class time, or to focus on a specific novel to learn in greater detail about a particular aspect of society. For example, the American frontier and western settlement are unique experiences which can be examined closely in many novels. The arrangement by theme *does not* include all of the novels in this book; it is intended to be suggestive, not exhaustive. Teachers may also wish to create additional themes or to modify existing themes.

Working by theme is an intriguing process; however, caution must be exercised. Grouping novels from the colonial period to the present under a particular theme can be an artificial exercise: It manipulates the novels and history. Use of the thematic grouping requires additional support from the teacher, other books or materials, and additional research by students. Otherwise, a tremendous amount of historical information will be left out, resulting in a distortion of history. On the other hand, thematic organization can be very useful. Long-range developments can be more easily grasped by students. Using one or two themes allows the student to organize simply a wide range of complex information. The arrangement by theme also reflects the multicultural character of America— there are themes on Native Americans, African Americans, and other immigrant groups.

The fourth list is a *title* index. All of the titles in the manual are arranged in alphabetical order. Each page on which a novel's title appears is listed. The page on which the annotation or descriptive summary appears is listed in **boldfaced** type.

Supplemental Listings

A supplemental movies listing near the end of the book identifies novels that have been made into films. Some teachers may wish to share this information with students; the pages are therefore designated as reproducible. Other teachers may wish to use the information on their own, either to recommend movies for student use or to watch for the student who decides to watch a movie instead of reading an assigned book.

Finally, the general index will make it easier to identify novels in which particular historical characters or events are featured, even if the novel does not focus solely on that event.

Awareness Levels and Point of View

Reading a novel is a complex process; a teacher should perhaps approach the novel by *awareness levels*. These levels depend on the reading level of individuals, small groups, or the class as a whole. The first level is an awareness of the plot line. Some novels deal with complicated historical events—which, when put into fictional form, can make it difficult for students to understand the story. The second level is an awareness of actual historical situations and how accurately they are portrayed in the novel. Students should be able to distinguish between the actual historical situations and the fictional historical situations. The third level is an awareness of what the characters represent or symbolize and their importance in terms of historical developments. For example, a character may represent a particular class structure, generational conflict, political corruption, or heroism in war. The fourth and final level is an awareness of abstract principles or philosophical content in the novel. Although this may be the author's ultimate goal in writing a novel, it may be possible—and even necessary—to discuss the novel without reaching this level. The teacher may have other purposes in mind in using the novel, and the reading level of the students may not be sufficiently developed to allow them to grasp abstract concepts. Many students will be unable to discuss a novel at a very abstract level, but they still will profit from reading it for its historical content. These awareness levels basically move on a continuum from simple to complex and may be used as a means of discussion or as the basis of various class exercises.

Reading novels also requires that teachers and students be aware of the *point of view* of the novelists and also of historians. Historians are required by their professional training to be as objective as possible in the gathering and writing of history. One of the historian's major goals is to present as closely as possible a narrative account of the truth—that which conforms to verifiable facts, based on primary and secondary sources. Historians who take up their tasks do so with a good reason or a great interest in their topic. Historians (like other people) are products of their times, and they reflect those times. Thus, historians bring some subjectivity or bias to their work. Even though students generally accept their textbooks as truthful or accurate, teachers should make students aware that history textbooks reflect the time period in which they were written and are written by people who make radical selections out of a vast amount of material. However, given that historians will have some degree of subjectivity in their presentation of historical circumstances, they still must seek to overcome overt bias. In short, professional historians must make every effort to adhere to factual information and empirical data.

Novelists have no such professional restrictions as the need for objectivity or constructing a truthful narrative. Novelists, who are also products of their times, have a point of view in creating their characters and constructing their plot lines. One particular way in which point of view has entered historians' and novelists' work is the critique of American historical figures, institutions, and values. Early in the twentieth century, novelists and historians who participated in this critique were called "muckrakers." Journalists and other writers also became muckrakers; all of these were people who found something they considered profoundly wrong in American society, or who wanted to correct accepted views of events and persons and then to report them. More recently, by the 1960's, writers who critiqued American society were called "debunkers." Some novels in this manual reflect muckraking and debunking. On the opposite side, many writers have no intent of critiquing American life; instead, they wish to extol or promote what would be considered a patriotic view—one that upholds accepted or traditional views of American historical figures, institutions, and values. Some novels, particularly from the Juvenile or Adolescent sections, reflect this intent. Teachers should carefully read the novels before use in class so they can be prepared to deal with the novelists' points of view.

Another way in which point of view enters the novel is through the novelists' treatment of women. Unfortunately, in the review of novels for this book, we found that many novelists (including many whom the literary establishment considers great "classical" American novelists) reflect sexism to a high degree. Sexism includes various types of situations. Women are brutalized in the novel, either by rape, beating, or murder; women are considered sexual objects only, existing in the novel merely as diversions or decorations for men; women's activities are considered insignificant; the plot revolves around men, and women play no role in motivating the plot; men demean the women by raping them, having inconsequential sex with them, leaving them to do what the men consider unimportant, or generally disregarding women's feelings or actions. Some novels that were too offensive in their sexism were not included. Some novels are important enough in their presentation of historical circumstances to be included despite their sexism. Novels that do reflect overt or extreme sexism are noted in the annotations.

In addition, point of view enters the novel in the author's treatment of racial and ethnic minorities. Many novels deal with the dozens of indigenous and immigrant groups who have contributed to American society. Some authors (especially of older novels) present situations or attitudes which contemporary Americans would consider racist or stereotypical. For example, some novels contain incidents or events that portray indigenous peoples only as savage enemies of white Europeans. More contemporary novels use the current designations of *Native American* or *American Indian,* explain the culture of various tribes, and indicate that white settlers also treated natives in particularly brutal fashion. Similarly, there are some authors who deal with African Americans in stereotypical patterns, such as conferring upon them lesser intelligence and abilities than whites. More modern authors utilize contemporary perspectives to show the effects of discrimination in education, occupations, and housing. Authors will use dialect to show the distinctness of Black English and its historical roots in the combination of African and southern American idioms. More African-American and Native-American authors are represented in novels written from the 1970's to the 1990's.

Where language or situations offensive to racial and ethnic minorities is present to an extreme degree or is overt, this is noted in the annotations. Foul language in some novels has also been noted in the annotations. Realism is present in many novels in the use of dialect or nonstandard English. Where especially noticeable, this is included in the annotations.

Sexism, racism, and prejudicial language may reflect realism from the novelists' point of view. They may also reflect what in contemporary opinion is a stereotypical or inaccurate representation of various groups in American society. Whatever the case may be, teachers should be aware of these elements in novels before they are presented to a class for study.

Novel Types

Also necessary is a note explaining the types of novels that are found in this manual: historical, biographical, classical, and utopian.

The first type is the *historical novel*. In the historical novel, actual historical circumstances and real characters drive the plot or are the reason for the plot; there are usually fictional characters introduced against the historical background. Such novelists often invent plausible conversations between characters. Historical novels are usually set in a time at least one generation prior to the authors' own times, although authors do also write legitimately on topics in contemporary history.

In the *biographical novel,* the main character of the biography drives the action; fictional characters are not usually introduced against the historical background. These novelists also often create plausible conversations between characters. Biographical novels are usually written a generation or more after the death of the subject of the biography— although again, biographers can write their stories of persons still living.

Classical novels are those that are judged by later generations to be masterpieces or worthy of veneration. These novels have served as standards, models, or guides to other authors. They usually adhere to an accepted set of standards or methods of writing, or they create new standards or methods. Classical novels are considered literary products of the first rank or definitive in the field.

Utopian novels are set in future times and imagined places.

All four types of novels are covered in this book. The vast majority of the entries are historical novels. There are a few biographical novels, mostly focusing on presidents and presidents' wives. There are some classical novels, such as those by James Fenimore Cooper and Nathaniel Hawthorne. And, there are a few utopian novels. The differences among these novels are not crucial to studying history, but teachers should make students aware of the variations. Introductions and explanatory notes included in the novels themselves often offer the best assistance in discerning the type of novel under study.

STUDENT ACTIVITIES

Both teacher and students need more than general discussions to incorporate novels into class work. At the end of this section are various activities which may be used effectively in classes. They include written, oral, and imaginative exercises, and projects that result in physical products; they can be done by individuals, groups, or the class as a whole; they take place in class and out of class. As with any activity, teachers will want to monitor student progress on a regular basis and set up schedules for completion. Some of the activities can involve the participation of other teachers; many of the activities might enlist the aid of parents or other supervising adults outside the classroom.

One of the best ways to keep students on task and on schedule is to set up a system of progress reports to be handed in to the teacher at regular intervals. For written projects, outlines, bibliographies, and rough drafts can be required at points before the final draft. For oral reports, a question sheet covering basic queries on sources, outline of the presentation, and time spent can be used. If students have any choice of topic, topic selection can be required by a certain date for approval. Teachers can use class time or activity time after school for short interviews with students on the status of projects. It is especially important for teachers to check on the progress of teams or groups to ensure that all persons are participating equally; be sure that tasks in groups are assigned to individuals so that each student has a clear idea of what is expected. Also, arrange grades so that each student receives a separate grade as well as a group grade.

All of the activities listed represent numerous ways in which students can be evaluated or graded—in addition to standard testing or daily recitation, which may make up the bulk of how students are graded. Teachers recognize that they can use alternate methods of evaluation because students' abilities and interests vary widely. Some students are simply better writers, or talkers, or more clever with their hands than others; various evaluation methods can address students' strengths and help improve performance overall.

Teachers can also plan activities according to a time frame. This would include planning daily, weekly, monthly, and unit activities. Teachers can also keep in mind the *placement* of activities. Some activities are good as introductory or initiatory. Others will serve as developmental, or those that are used as the unit progresses. And, many activities fit nicely as ending or culminating activities. Learning outcomes or objectives should always be kept in mind as activities are planned. Teachers are always aware that activities should result in the acquisition or examination of knowledge, skills, attitudes, and values.

Teachers can choose among several approaches when planning activities. These approaches include an emphasis on personalities in novels, an examination of issues or points of debate which novels bring out, the development of themes or concepts in novels which pervade or recur over a period of time (see Arrangement III: Themes), or the recognition of problems or perplexing questions brought forward for solutions in the novels. Each of these approaches can appeal to students in a variety of ways, but all can be used to stimulate curiosity and learning.

The following is a list of suggested activities:

1. Assign one or more of the following questions for written work or class discussions:
    a. Are historical circumstances specifically mentioned? What are they? What does the author say about them?
    b. What social classes and educational backgrounds are involved?
    c. What values or value systems do the characters reflect or represent?
    d. Are the principal characters part of the socioeconomic background or are they outsiders?
    e. Are characters broken by the system, or do they gain entrance to it?
    f. What in the author's own background influenced the writing?
    g. If the author wrote during the time period of the novel, what conclusions can you draw about the author's attitude toward his or her own times?
    h. Is the author biased or impartial in his or her presentation of the times and the characters?
    i. Is the author representative of, or contrary to, the values of the time period?
2. Assign papers dealing with one of the themes in Arrangement III. These themes should force students to reflect upon and research a subject that covers a long time period.
3. Have students invent an imaginary conversation using the characters from one novel or from different novels in different time periods. The conversation can be free-flowing, or it can focus on the characters' imaginary reactions to specific questions or a theme. The characters can be actual historical figures, or imaginary characters, or both. The conversation can be oral or written.
4. Select scenes with historical content from various novels. Have students then script, direct, produce, and present the scenes to the class. If possible, videotape the scenes. Invite speech- or drama-department members to offer advice and to view the presentations.
5. Assign two or more students to the same novel and have them handle different questions from activity 1. Or, assign two or more students to the same theme but have them read different novels. Have these groups participate in panel discussions in front of the class or in small-group discussions.
6. Have each student write a directed journal that records political, social, economic, and ethical-philosophical factors that are encountered while reading. Collect the journals periodically and show students how a journal can be used as a resource for book reports, discussions, oral reports, papers, or exams.
7. Have students write an extension of the novel. That is, after the novel ends, have students put the characters in other situations that might logically occur. This shows whether students have grasped the historical content of the novel and can translate this by making the characters do other things in new situations.
8. Have students write "slices of life" or "daily life" essays that are fictional accounts of people who could have actually lived. These can be based on life described in a novel and other class-text work. This should involve substantial

research by a student. The student can write about a day, a month, or several years in the lifetime of a character.

9. Set up discussions or workshops where students discuss the differences and similarities between history and literature. How does a historian deal with historical information as compared with—or contrasted to—how a novelist handles literary detail?

10. Have students interview characters from the novels in a "You Are There" format organized around a theme.

11. Have students make tabletop scenes from the novels. These can include famous battles; architectural examples, such as forts or buildings; or settings that are appropriate for models such as forests, towns, or cities. For novels with future or utopian settings, making a model of the possible setting would be intriguing.

12. Assign individuals or groups to make bulletin boards on particular aspects of the novels or related aspects. Geographical bulletin boards work well: trace a journey, show the geographical aspects of a region, or map the town. Bulletin boards might be used to show family genealogies or aspects of a presidency.

13. Have students who are artistically talented draw illustrations of important or especially vivid scenes to accompany the text. Students could model illustrations on those often found in the novels, or they could create their own styles. Many characters lend themselves very well to cartooning.

14. If there is a collection available, students might look through late-nineteenth-century and early-twentieth-century magazines or newspapers (some public libraries keep these on microfilm) to study fashion, advertisements, and typical activities of the period. Students might keep scrapbooks of collected copies of fashions and advertisements. They might also create montages or collages (artistically arranged pictures, advertisements, etc., on poster board or bulletin boards) from collected samples.

15. Many of these novels have been filmed, some specifically for television and many as commercial (major motion picture) movies. Many older movies can be obtained through film catalogues, the public library, or video stores. It might be worthwhile to show films and compare/contrast them with the novels from which they were adapted.

16. Since many of the novels deal with family histories, some students might be interested in exploring their own family histories in an informal way through available relatives, keepsakes, antiques, photo albums, diaries, Bibles, etc. What has influenced students in their lives? This theme is often explored in the novels. Since many students will have an Asian, African, or European ethnic origin, they may become more interested in immigration, immigration patterns, and current immigration problems.

17. If there is a museum nearby, take students to the museum to study paintings, sculptures, or physical remains of various periods that correspond to periods in selected novels. How are women, men, and children portrayed in art of different periods? Judging from the artistic examples, what do students think these societies have valued?

18. Invite speakers into the class to speak on particular aspects of the novels. These can be people who have an interest or expertise in such topics as Native American history; the Revolutionary War; the Civil War; World War I or World War II; the Korean War; the Vietnam War; experience in movements such as civil rights for Native Americans, women, or blacks; examples of professionals such as doctors, lawyers, writers, businesspeople; local museum curators or directors.

19. Have students interview family members, friends, or other people who have had military experience. Since this has played such a large role in American history, it is important for students to know the effects of military life on participants.

20. Historical sites are plentiful throughout America. Plan a trip or trips to sites that are reflected in novels. Teachers have enough choice among novels to select one in their region: Revolutionary or Civil War battlefields; historic homes; industrial buildings, ports, rivers, and canals; Native American reservations or former tribal territory; colonial era re-creations; or historic districts in cities are among the many possibilities for trips.

21. Arrange to see plays based on events in a novel or the era in which the novel takes place.

22. Plan to have students switch roles to see how various patterns have worked their way through American life. This activity has to be planned, explained, and supervised carefully. For example, have whites and African Americans reverse roles; have boys and girls assume the role of the opposite sex; have students assume other minority roles, such as Asians or Hispanics. This activity can be very limited—such as white students discussing the legal restrictions placed on them if they were blacks in the 1950's, including the use of public transportation, segregation in schools, and barriers to voting. This activity can also be very involved—for example, students could be required to "live" in their assumed roles for a period of time in and out of the classroom. Extended participation in this activity must be carefully monitored.

23. Have students read novels carefully to look for descriptions of what people ate in bygone eras. With the teacher's help in finding recipes (often available in period cookbooks or on site in living-history projects), students could make Native American, colonial, and nineteenth-century vegetable and meat dishes, breads, and desserts.

24. Have students produce a living-history project by re-creating clothing, tools, rooms, furniture, and other items and settings from a particular novel and then inviting other classes for a demonstration.

25. Have students interview elderly family members, friends, or even residents of nursing homes for reminiscences of earlier eras covered in the novels. For example, they could ask what life was like without television sets, airplanes, modern appliances, or automobiles; what people did for leisure activities; what schooling was like; how they survived the Depression; how the present compares with their childhood pasts. This will often give students an even closer look into an era depicted in a novel.

26. Have students "update" historical situations encountered in the novels by studying what is occurring in the present. Pioneer, farm, rural, town, and city life provide the settings for many novels. Visit a modern farm to see how technology

and business have changed farm life; visit a modern city and the historic district of the city to see how the city has changed; look at old photographs of towns and cities to see what alterations have occurred; investigate the status of the current civil rights and women's rights movements; compare native tribes of the nineteenth century with their modern tribal counterparts. Nearly all of these groups, institutions, or settings have their own organizations which keep historic records.

27. Have students investigate the costs of items and services mentioned in the novel, such as food; clothing; furniture; tools; transportation; education; doctors' and lawyers' fees; restaurant prices; houses; animals used on the farm; books and newspapers; items such as eyeglasses, watches, false teeth, and kitchen appliances. Costs are often mentioned in novels; period newspapers and magazines contain advertisements as do old mail-order catalogues. Older relatives and friends are also good sources. Compare costs to today's living expenses, and have students make up yearly household budgets for pioneer and farm families or city dwellers. Compare those costs to yearly wages for various jobs and professions. The U.S. Labor Department has records on wages for occupations that go back several decades.

28. Have students read newspaper opinion-editorial pages of local, regional, or national newspapers. Many of these are kept on microfilm at local or college libraries. Reading editorials, essays, and columns of the time period can give students good insight into public opinion of the times. Students can compare past opinions to opinions on parallel events today—for movements such as civil rights and women's rights; for events such as wars; or for serious national disasters such as floods, droughts, and storms often mentioned in novels.

29. Have students create a newspaper reflecting a town or city that is the center of the novel under study or reflecting major persons and events of the novel. The newspaper can include headline stories on the major events; feature articles on the major characters; and an opinion-editorial page which reflects issues in the novel.

30. Create versions of the *Jeopardy* and Trivial Pursuit games which cover major events, issues, and personalities of a novel. This approach would work well with longer novels and those that cover significant events such as the Revolutionary and Civil Wars. Students can master much factual material in this manner, research and write the categories and questions themselves, and organize into teams for the games. Prizes can be awarded for winning teams.

31. If students are reading a novel that takes place in your region, city, or town, have them do a "Tour-a-Town," "Tour-a-City," or "Tour-a-Region" research project. This can include descriptions of the history of the relevant region, city, or town; biographies of significant persons; a geographic orientation; important events; highlights for today's visitors; a visit by the mayor; and packets of pictures, brochures, and maps.

32. In some instances, it might be possible to have the author or illustrator of a novel come to your school. This requires a commitment of time and resources by the school, but it can be made into a schoolwide and community event. An author can talk about researching the book, personal experiences, life as a

writer, or development of the novel. An illustrator can do some artwork as part of the presentation and explain the development of the illustrations in the novel.

33. Since many novels involve adolescents and younger children, investigate games of the period of a novel under study. Sometimes these are mentioned in the novel. Other likely sources are the local historical museum, mail-order catalogues, and elderly persons. Materials for games can be gathered or made and the games played as part of regular recreation periods.

34. Ask students whom they admire or respect in the novel or whom they would want to be or be like. Have them support their answers. They can even talk in character or dress in character. Conversely, ask students whom they dislike or have little respect for in the novel and why. This gives students a chance to think about character, values, morals, and judgment.

35. Engage the students in a "Time Travel" exercise by imagining themselves back in the time period of a novel and altering events. This gives students insight into both the historical events under study and the novelist's creative activity.

36. Engage the students in a discussion of "What would happen if . . .?" a character lived, or died, or events occurred differently. This gives students a chance to examine motivations of characters, the logic or chance of historical events, and the impact of persons on events.

37. If you are in a school that has continuing or adult education or is near a college or university, you might be able to have a demonstration of pottery making or even have students make some of their own pottery. Pottery is a significant symbol and reflection of time periods. You might also be able to arrange demonstrations of candle making, weaving and dyeing cloth, making iron implements, etc. All of these reflect the material culture of periods under study.

38. Many communities have retained or re-created the one-room schoolhouse of a past era, complete with supplies and the teacher. If one of these is in your area, arrange a visit to see how learning occurred in this setting.

39. Many people live near depositories of original documents important in American history and the novels. These range from the Declaration of Independence and the Constitution to treaties with native tribes and foreign countries to speeches of presidents and significant persons. Arrange to see documents that are stored in your area.

40. Graveyards of all sizes are a significant reflection of many characteristics of a period. Gravestones can be investigated for prominent families, mortality rates, family size, indications of wealth, military history, disease and epidemics, and (in the East, particularly) how old the gravestones are. Some larger cemeteries may have guides who can give help in mapping out the graveyard.

41. Letter writing is almost a lost art, but one that was practiced widely until the contemporary era. Have students pick out a character or characters in the novel. They can write letters to the character about events and people in the novel, or they can write letters between characters in the novel.

42. Prepare five to ten short questions about key terms, places, or events for each day's recitation, discussion, or lecture. At the end of the period, ask students the questions for a quick check on memory or comprehension.

43. When students are reading a novel that takes place in a prominent city or region outside of your area or even near your area, have them prepare an imaginary trip to the place. This would involve sending for information, visiting the local travel agency, investigating transportation, deciding on costs, and arranging how time would be spent in the place to be toured. This activity can serve as an "update" activity; it gives students an idea of how places have changed and how the history of a place has affected both the site and its people. It also spurs interest in the possibility of a real visit at some future time.

44. Many novels have important Americans such as presidents, politicians, military heroes, or cultural figures who play significant roles—or who serve as reference points—in the novel. Have students research and prepare biographies of selected actual persons in the novel and present them to the class. This can be a good team activity.

45. America has always been a culturally diverse country. Many of the novels deal with immigrants from Europe, Asia, and Latin America. Investigate various languages from cultural groups covered in selected novels, and arrange for language demonstrations in your class. This type of activity can also include demonstrations of food, holiday customs, clothing and costumes, and religions represented by the various ethnic groups. Students with appropriate backgrounds can do the demonstrations, visitors can be brought in, or the class can work in teams on these activities to reflect aspects of culture.

46. Many of the novels deal with pioneering and frontier life from the earliest colonists on the East Coast to the pioneers who closed the western frontier by 1890. Much happened to the natural surroundings on the continent, including deforestation, building of farmsteads and large farms, creating national parks, ranching, and providing for water. Have students investigate what has happened to the natural surroundings in their area since the time period of a novel under study. Did the novelist have a point of view about nature and the relationship between people and nature? What is the current status of the environment in your area compared with its status in the time period of the novel under study?

47. There will be several students in any class who are good writers. Some may wish to write their own short stories or even "mini-novels" based on events or characters in a novel—or based on events and people in their families' pasts. Encourage students to participate in this kind of writing, which can be done even on the middle-school level.

48. Medicine and medical practices can fascinate students of all ages. Investigate medicines, treatments, doctors, and medical training of the time period of the novel under study. Compare these with medical practices and medicines of natives or other cultures or with medicine of today.

49. Most schools will be equipped with word processors or computers. Many activities can be planned using this equipment—including writing projects, keeping track of characters and plot lines, making up the various game-type activities mentioned earlier, plotting geographical routes, keeping genealogy charts, and many other projects.

50. A debate is always a popular and useful activity. Form debate teams on issues relating to the Revolution, Civil War and other wars, civil rights, the environment, business practices, or any other issue that is prominent or acts as the center of a novel under study.

51. During the colonial era, the frontier period, and other times, creating rules and regulations or laws became very important to people. Have students create sets of laws or rules of conduct for a colonial society, a western frontier town, a "big business" of the nineteenth century, or any other period which is under study in a given novel.

Arrangement I:

Annotated Bibliography

JUDITH MACBAIN ALTER (1938–   )
Luke and the Van Zandt County War (1984; 130 PAGES; E/E)

Fourteen-year-old Theo Burford moves in 1867 from Mississippi to Texas with her widowed father, a physician. Luke Widman, a neighbor boy abandoned by his father, comes to live with the Burfords. Political upheaval occurs when citizens of Van Zandt County agitate for secession from the state of Texas and the federal government. Theo and her father are opposed to violence and the secession, while Luke and the rest of the county favor a war for the county's independence. Finally, after raids and a lynching by the Ku Klux Klan, and Luke's narrow escape from federal troops, he joins the Burfords in opposing secession. All learn about individual responsibility in government during this harrowing experience of mob mentality in the Van Zandt County War, a little-known historical incident.

SHERWOOD ANDERSON (1876–1941)
Poor White (1920; 363 PAGES; M/M)

Poor White is primarily a criticism of the exploitative aspects of industrialism. During the 1880's to 1920's, Hugh McVey, living in poverty, is desperate to escape the idle and useless lifestyle of his drunken father. Eventually settling in the agrarian community of Bidwell, Ohio, Hugh is frustrated by his inability to be noticed. He begins to invent and build time- and work-saving farm machinery. A self-serving townsman promotes Hugh's inventions, and soon the quiet town is dotted with factories. Hugh realizes that the once close-knit community has been transformed by greed, false pride, and a loss of humanity. In a town where once there was a work ethic based on pride and workmanship, there are now factory workers, exploited and angry that they are spending their lives making the factory owners and "money men" richer.

HARRIETTE ARNOW (1908–1986)
The Dollmaker (1954; 549 PAGES; D/D)

The lure of high-paying wartime jobs is the focus of this novel. Gertie Nevels scrimps and saves for the day when she and her family can buy the farmland they want in Ballew, Kentucky. But it is the 1940's, World War II is going on, and Gertie's husband has other ideas. He wants to move instead to Detroit, where he believes big money can be made working in armament factories. Although neither Gertie nor the children want to rent in Detroit when they could have their own farm, Gertie dutifully follows her husband. Moving from open space and fresh air to government tract housing leaves Gertie miserable. Her only consolation is her hobby of whittling, from which she makes dolls, crucifixes, and, most importantly, a bust of Christ. Gertie knows that when the war ends, so does her husband's job. He, however, cannot imagine a time when men stop making things to kill other men.

HARRIETTE ARNOW (1908–1986)
The Kentucky Trace (1974; 286 PAGES; M/M)

The American Revolution is the historical setting for this story. Leslie Collins, a surveyor by profession, is fighting on the rebel side. He is captured by bandits and then rescued by mountain men. Collins later makes his way home—to find it deserted and his family gone. He follows his one clue down the Kentucky Trace trail where he meets a number of people: an old woodsman, a slave girl, a young Indian, and a woman unconcerned with saving her baby's life. The main focus then shifts to Collins's attempt to save the child.

HELEN TANN ASCHMANN
Connie Bell, M.D. (1963; 301 PAGES; M/M)

In the late nineteenth century, the education of female doctors was just beginning. The first class of Chicago's Women's Medical College was graduated in 1871. Fictional Connie Bell is created against this historical background as one of the first graduates. Supported by her physician grandfather and her teachers, Connie must still make her way alone in a tough field. She survives a riot against the "female doctor impersonators" and the Chicago fire in order to prove that she is truly a professional. This could be read as an early attempt to create role-model novels for girls.

MARGARET ATWOOD (1939–   )
The Handmaid's Tale (1986; 395 PAGES; D/D)

The life of Offred the Handmaid can be read as the culmination of 1970's–1990's conservative opinions on the role of women, carried to an extreme. The Republic of Gilead (the futuristic United States) is a country run by dictatorial men with philosophies that stress an inferior position of women in the disguise of stressing the significance of family and children. Although Offred has memories of an earlier, freer life, she finds herself a nonperson whose only value depends on her ability to bear children. She plots to escape from Gilead and records her struggle in the hope of reaching other women. Her records are discovered, but her fate is left to the reader to imagine. This novel includes background material on women's issues and legislation affecting women's legal, social, and economic positions.

AVI (1937–   )
Encounter at Easton (1980; 133 PAGES; E/E)

In the early eighteenth century, Elizabeth Mawes and Robert Linnly, young indentured servants, run away and make their way north into Easton Township, Pennsylvania. At the time of this story indenturing servants is a common practice. Lured by the hope of jobs, security, and freedom, the two find a tragic end to their journey. Elizabeth falls gravely ill and is cared for by a mysterious woman; Robert is offered work—but by a person who is pursuing them. The story is told in the format of court testimony given by Robert and three men who were part of the events. Thus, the tale unfolds as a series of flashbacks in the first person.

AVI (1937–   )
The Fighting Ground (1984; 152 PAGES; E/E)

During the Revolutionary War, thirteen-year-old Jonathan wants desperately to fight the British and their allies, the German Hessians. His father does not want him to go to war. When Jonathan is sent to see why an alarm has sounded near his home, he runs off to join the war instead of returning home. Captured by Hessian soldiers, Jonathan does not understand their language, or why they do not kill him. In a conflict with American soldiers, the Hessians are mercilessly slaughtered. When the Americans boast to local citizens and other soldiers of their bravery and "victory" over the hapless Hessians, Jonathan stops considering war exciting and glorious. He finally understands his father's loathing of war as his own life is forever altered by this brief experience.

BETTY BAKER (1928–   )
Walk the World's Rim (1965; 168 PAGES; E/E)

The southern rim of the present-day United States is the setting for this early-sixteenth-century adventure of Spanish explorers, a black slave, and Indians. A Spanish expedition lands in Florida, and all but four of its members eventually perish: three Spaniards and a black slave, Esteban. These four wander west for years; along the way, they meet various southern Indian tribes. One of these tribes, the Avavares, take them in and send one of their young men, Chakoh, along on a trip to Mexico. There, the Spaniards hope to be rewarded for their efforts. Their journeys reveal much about Indian life in the southern borderlands in the sixteenth century.

DON BANNISTER (1928–)
Long Day at Shiloh (1981; 272 PAGES; M/M)

In a long series of short, sharp vignettes—or brief word pictures—the first twenty-four hours of the Battle of Shiloh take place. The time is from midnight, April 5, to midnight, April 6, 1862; the place is Pittsburgh Landing on the Tennessee River. From the viewpoints of both Union Army General Ulysses Grant and ordinary Union soldiers, the twenty-four hours elapse. Grant's officers play cards; recruits drink through the night; Grant plans the following day; the unexpected attack occurs; men flee, are wounded, and die; acts of bravery and cowardice occur. The style makes this a personal story.

SHIRLEY BARKER (1911–1965)
The Road to Bunker Hill (1962; 178 PAGES; E/E)

Tension is rising in 1770's Newburyport, Charlestown, and Bunker Hill, Massachusetts, as the American Revolution unfolds. The events that are about to occur will change the young lives of Kitty Greenleaf, her cousin Sally Rose, Tom Trask, and Gerald Malory. The British pick Bunker Hill as the site of the first major engagement of the Revolution. Tom goes off to join his native New Hampshire regiment and to participate in the battle. The girls help Granny Greenleaf run the tavern, where there are still many British soldiers. Gerald Malory, as Sally finds out much later, is merely play-acting as a British solider. All of the characters play parts in the early drama of the Revolution.

CAPTAIN EDWARD BEACH (1918–)
Run Silent, Run Deep (1955; 364 PAGES; M/D)

In 1941, when Japanese war fleets are a dangerous force, U.S. Navy Commander Edward Richardson is skipper of a World War II submarine. Leaning heavily on naval terminology, the fictional Richardson recounts the events leading up to his being awarded the Congressional Medal of Honor. Patrolling the Pacific waterways searching for vessels, the Navy is confounded by the scope of knowledge of "Bungo Pete," a Japanese destroyer skipper. Richardson discovers that Bungo Pete gains his "secret" information by combing through garbage thrown from U.S. Navy ships. Cracking this mystery, Richardson goes on to destroy Bungo Pete. In so doing, he murders innocent Japanese citizens who are being carried in three lifeboats. Agonizing over his actions, Richardson does not recover until after he helps save a ship from Japanese air attack.

PATRICIA BEATTY (1922–1991)
Be Ever Hopeful, Hannalee (1988; 207 PAGES; E/E)

Poor whites and newly freed blacks struggle to build new lives in post-Civil-War Atlanta in 1865. Many former plantation owners also struggle to rebuild their lives. Young Hannalee Reed and her black friend Delie live in poor shantytowns at opposite ends of town from each other. Both work at menial jobs, struggling to raise themselves and their families out of poverty. The author's note following this novel discusses the historical facts of the period. Included are the condition of postwar Atlanta, the rise of the Ku Klux Klan, the fall of plantations, the status of blacks after the abolition of slavery, and a general history of Georgia from 1788 through 1976.

PATRICIA BEATTY (1922–1991)
Charley Skedaddle (1987; 180 PAGES; E/E)

Street gangs have been a factor in big-city life for many years. In the 1860's, twelve-year-old Charley Quinn is a member of the Bowery Boys' street gang in New York City. His sister financially supports both him and her fiancé. Charley's brother has been killed in the Civil War; Charley decides to take his dead brother's place in the Union Army. Taken on as a drummer boy because of his youth, Charley nonetheless shoots a rebel soldier and then deserts, or "skedaddles." Lost in the Blue Ridge Mountains of Virginia, Charley is taken in by an old woman. Working for her, Charley finds appreciation for the southern mountains and their peoples. Charley finds worth in himself, even if he did "skedaddle" from the war.

PATRICIA BEATTY (1922–1991)
Eight Mules from Monterey (1982; 181 PAGES; E/E)

In 1916, the time of this story, California still reflects many aspects of the pioneer West: isolated mountain areas, lack of communications, people cut off from events of the outside world. Fayette Ashmore, her brother Eubie, and her librarian mother set out to establish branch library outposts in the areas around Monterey. No small feat, this experience takes them, by mule, into territory without any roads and into contact with eccentric mountain people—including "moonshiners" (people making whiskey illegally). Based on a real librarian who established library outposts in the area, this story also draws on Beatty's own extensive background as a librarian and student of the American West.

Patricia Beatty (1922–1991)
Hail Columbia (1970; 232 pages; m/m)

Louisa's aunt, Columbia Baines, arrives in Astoria, Oregon, in 1893 and proceeds to upset the town and her family because of her ideas. Aunt Columbia is a suffragette, or a supporter of women having the vote; she is used to chaining herself to public buildings to advance the cause. Columbia also embraces other causes: the immigrant Finns, the despised Chinese, getting rid of corrupt politicians at city hall, temperance rallies. Astoria, Oregon, actually exists, and Beatty bases her action on incidents reported in the contemporary newspapers of the time. Beatty also does a great deal to debunk the myth that suffragettes were neurotic, man-hating shrews. Instead, the vast majority were well educated, from supportive families, and very courageous in the face of physical threats.

Patricia Beatty (1922–1991)
How Many Miles to Sundown (1974; 206 pages; e/e)

Three young people journey through Texas and the New Mexico and Arizona Territories in the late 1880's. Nate Graber is searching for his father. His companions are brother and sister Leo and Beeler Quimey. Beeler, a girl of thirteen who is the chief character, is accompanied by her pet longhorn steer, Travis. Along their adventure-filled routes, the three young people encounter people and circumstances true to the life of this period. They meet Billy the Kid, spend some time with a traveling circus, learn about mining, and realize what a great new thing the railroad will be.

Patricia Beatty (1922–1991)
Jayhawker (1991; 202 pages; m/m)

In 1861, when Missouri secedes from the Union, young Lije Tulley and his family live across the state border in Kansas. Lije and his brother are "Jayhawkers," a term describing Kansas abolitionists who cross into Missouri to free slaves. After Lije's father is killed by a Missouri slaveholder during a failed rescue attempt, Lije becomes a spy for the Union and lives under an assumed name in Missouri. A frequent companion in Missouri is Jim Hickok, known later as Wild Bill Hickok. Unknown at first to Lije, Hickok is also a spy for the Union. Lije's cover is blown when he accompanies Confederate raiders to Lawrence, Kansas, where Lije's mother owns a business. Facing down the Missourian who killed his father, Lije momentarily considers shooting him, but decides there has been too much death in this movement already. The antislavery martyr John Brown plays a prominent role in this story, and other well-known names in American history make appearances as well. An author's note contains many valuable facts on the history of Missouri and Kansas during this period.

PATRICIA BEATTY (1922–1991)
Just Some Weeds from the Wilderness (1978; 236 PAGES; M/M)

This story is loosely based on the life of Lydia Pinkham, a businesswoman and women's rights champion who actually lived in Massachusetts in the late nineteenth century. Adelina Westlake lives in Oregon during the same period. Attempting to save her family from bankruptcy in the panic of 1873, Adelina concocts a folk remedy, and, with the help of her niece Lucinda, she successfully markets "Mrs. Westlake's Wonder-Working Elixir." Even though it is unheard of for women to go into business for themselves in this period—or allow their likenesses to appear in advertising—Adelina does both. In addition, she becomes interested in working conditions of women and in women's rights. These themes are woven into the setting of Portland and Willamette Valley in pioneer days.

PATRICIA BEATTY (1922–1991)
Lupita Mañana (1981; 177 PAGES; M/M)

Not set in the past, this is nonetheless a novel that reflects a long-standing historical problem between Mexico and the United States: illegal immigrants. Thirteen-year-old Lupita Mañana and her brother, Salvador, leave Mexico and enter the U.S. after their father dies and they must find work. They find their way to relatives in California, but they are constantly fearful of being discovered and deported even after obtaining agricultural jobs. Beatty attacks several concerns: the open borders of two democratic countries, working conditions in agricultural jobs for immigrants, youngsters who must become independent and work, the operation of U.S. immigration laws and the Immigration and Naturalization Service, the lure of a new prosperous culture, and the necessity to learn English in the new society. This is well researched and based on the experiences of actual persons.

PATRICIA BEATTY (1922–1991)
Something to Shout About (1976; 240 PAGES; M/M)

This is the story of some very capable nineteenth-century women. Thirteen-year-old Hope Foster and her family are participants in the birth of a new town, Ottenberg, in the Montana Territory in 1875. Hope's father owns the general store; the family is used to moving from one mining town to another. However, Ottenberg experiences some unusual events. First, a young medical student boarding with the Fosters turns out to be a woman. Then, the women of the town begin to canvass the many saloons to get donations for a new school. A female lawyer and female newspaper writer aid the women in their quest. The doctor, lawyer, and newswriter are all based on actual characters who lived in the area during that period. Interestingly, it was not unusual for women to disguise themselves as men in order to enter professions.

PATRICIA BEATTY (1922–1991)
That's One Ornery Orphan (1980; 205 PAGES; M/M)

The casual adoption practices for orphans in Texas in the 1870's provide the main focus in the story of Hallie Lee Baker. In an age when little charity and few laws existed regarding the poor and orphaned, Hallie Lee's orphan home was all too common. Her experiences in trying to be adopted lead to three unsuccessful attempts: a fire-and-brimstone preacher, a country doctor, and a traveling actress. Along the way, Beatty weaves in late-nineteenth-century topics of how orphans were selected and treated, the cowboy versus the farmer, the preacher and camp meetings, medical practices, life on the stage, and the role of immigrants in Texas life. This is a story told with some pathos and much humor.

PATRICIA BEATTY (1922–1991)
Wait for Me, Watch for Me, Eula Bee (1978; 203 PAGES; E/E)

The author provides much insight into the lives of the Comanche and Kiowa Indians in this story. Lewallen and Eula Bee, the only survivors of a Comanche raid, are taken as captives by the Indians in Texas during the Civil War. With the rest of the family dead or in the Confederate Army, Lewallen must bear the responsibility for his life and his sister's. Lewallen escapes from the Comanches and meets a former neighbor named Cabral, who was distrusted by the Bee family. However, Cabral's children have also been captured, so Lewallen and Cabral form a plan to free their relatives. In this period, west Texas was unprotected due to the war; thus Comanches and Kiowa Indians held considerable power in the area.

JOHN (1922–1975) AND PATRICIA BEATTY (1922–1991)
Who Comes to King's Mountain? (1975; 264 PAGES; M/M)

Most Americans of Scottish heritage were on the side of the British in the Revolutionary War, despite Britain's treatment of Scotland earlier in the century. In 1780, fourteen-year-old Alexander MacLeod of South Carolina faces a choice. Alex decides he must take up the colonists' side. In less than a year, he is fighting along the Atlantic coast with Francis Marion—the "Swamp Fox." Fearful of the return of the British and certain officers who are known to be cruel, Alex prepares for his moment as a soldier. He participates in the Battle of Camden and then in the battle at King's Mountain, which proves to be a turning point in the war.

LORNA BEERS (1897–   )
The Crystal Cornerstone (1953; 218 PAGES; M/M)

In 1776, the Declaration of Independence stirs thoughts of liberty, freedom, and citizens' rights in all patriots' minds. Sixteen-year-old Thaddeus Long, who lives in Pennsylvania, longs to go off to fight for these principles. But his family intends that he should enroll in the College of New Jersey at Prince Town. Carried away by excitement, Thaddeus instead joins a group of Liberty Boys—in reality a mob, who tar and feather a neighbor who will not give up his goods for the rebel cause. Ashamed of his actions, Thaddeus decides to run off and join Washington's forces. He is introduced to the realities of battle conditions and learns what the war really means.

KENSIL BELL
Jersey Rebel (1963; 248 PAGES; M/M)

British General Howe occupied Philadelphia in 1777, and thus placed the revolutionary struggle in great danger. Using actual dispatches, diaries, and journals of British and American citizens of that era, the author builds the framework of the attempt to dislodge Howe's army. Fictional fourteen-year-old Jeff Lundy lives across the Delaware River in New Jersey, a few miles below Philadelphia. Dismayed by the occupation, he joins in the land and naval forces' attempts to blockade Howe's army into starvation. Generals Washington and Lafayette and the battles at Forts Mercer and Mifflin play a part in the story.

NATHANIEL BENCHLEY (1915–1981)
Only Earth and Sky Last Forever (1972; 189 PAGES; E/E)

A treaty signed in 1868 promised that the Black Hills area of the Dakota Territory would remain Indian land. Dark Elk is a Cheyenne Indian brought up by the Oglala Sioux since the age of twelve, when U.S. army raids killed his parents. He lives for a time on a reservation, but, frustrated and wanting to become a warrior, he goes off in search of Chief Crazy Horse. The whites have now begun to invade the Black Hills. Dark Elk participates in skirmishes and battles against the army. Finally, he takes part in the Indian victory at the great Battle of the Little Bighorn in 1876. In the end, however, Dark Elk knows that freedom for the American Indians is over.

NATHANIEL BENCHLEY (1915–1981)
Portrait of a Scoundrel (1979; 298 PAGES; M/M)

Portrait of a Scoundrel is the account of the life of a little-known character in American history: James Greenleaf. Benchley uses Greenleaf's letters, letters of his brother, and other sources to re-create the life of a typical speculator in the decades after the American Revolution. In this boisterous and creative period, Greenleaf's life in Boston, Philadelphia, and Washington, D.C., intersects with the lives of George Washington, John Adams, and Aaron Burr. Greenleaf observes events from extreme vantage points—from the highest circles of political power to the depths of a debtor's prison. This story is told with considerable humor.

TED BIRKMAN
To Seize the Passing Dream (1972; 416 PAGES; D/D)

James McNeill Whistler (1834–1903) was an American who lived in St. Petersburg, Russia, as a boy. He went to West Point (following family tradition), and spent his art-student days in Paris. This biographical novel follows Whistler's career and his personal life through all of these events. In addition, his nearly forty years in London, his relationships with his mistresses and his wife, and his interaction with his mother—who becomes the subject of Whistler's most famous painting—are catalogued. A flamboyant man, Whistler comes into contact with artists of the day, including Degas, Monet, Toulouse-Lautrec, and Sargent. Always in need of money and not achieving recognition until late in life, Whistler refuses to alter his style and stamps his genius on an era.

JOAN W. BLOS (1928–)
A Gathering of Days (1979; 139 PAGES; E/E)

This novel, in journal format, recounts fourteen-year-old Catherine Hall's memories of two years, from 1830 to 1832. She lives with her widowed father and younger sister on a farm in New Hampshire. The period during which she keeps the journal becomes one of the most important of her life. Her father remarries, and his new wife brings a stepbrother into the house. Catherine and her best friend, Cassie, help a runaway slave survive through the winter, although they never actually see him. Cassie also dies during this period, and Catherine is jolted into a grownup world. As she recounts events, Catherine also reveals aspects of everyday life: school, harvesting, quilting, berrying, and changes of season in New England.

LARRY BOGRAD (1953–)
Los Alamos Light (1983; 168 PAGES; E/E)

In 1943, sixteen-year-old Maggie Chilton's world changes on the day her atomic-scientist father announces they are moving to New Mexico. Maggie's new home, in Los Alamos, is in the middle of a desert and consists mainly of government laboratories. Maggie feels isolated until she makes friends with local Native Americans and comes to cherish their land. Maggie learns to enjoy her new life and to understand the importance of her father's work. Helping Dr. Oppenheimer perfect the world's first atomic bomb, Maggie's father contributes to the Japanese surrender, which is precipitated by the dropping of the first atomic bombs on Hiroshima and Nagasaki. The book explores the use of scientific research used to produce weapons.

CAROLE BOLTON (1926–)
Never Jam Today (1971; 241 PAGES; M/M)

In the early twentieth century, when women are still considered the property of men, seventeen-year-old Maddy Franklin wants a different life from that of her mother's generation. In the World War I era, she becomes involved in the woman suffrage movement, believing that women need the vote to control their destinies. With her mother, father, and boyfriend opposed, she becomes a suffragist and goes to prison twice for picketing the White House. The cruelty and unfairness suffragists endure at the hands of a "democratic" system eventually persuades Maddy's mother to join the movement, although her father remains opposed to women's rights. Struggling to acquire an education reserved mostly for men and to find her place in the world, Maddy is torn by her desire to marry her antisuffrage boyfriend.

NANCY BOND (1945–)
The Voyage Begun (1981; 316 PAGES; M/M)

Set on Cape Cod, Massachusetts, in the not-too-distant future, this novel depicts what life could be like when the nation's supply of energy runs out. Paul, his sister, Katie, and his father (who is a government research scientist) try to find answers to the puzzle of why their way of life—and life around them—are crumbling. Paul's father believes new technology will provide answers to what he considers to be short-term problems. Paul's sister thinks the problems will be much longer-lasting and difficult to resolve. The family are joined in their debate by a trio of other characters who represent different lifestyles forced on them by changes in their living environment.

FRANK BONHAM (1914–   )
The Ghost Front (1968; 212 PAGES; M/M)

The last major German offensive battle of World War II occurred on the German-Belgian border in the Ardennes Forest region; it is commonly known as the Battle of the Bulge. In December 1944, eighteen-year-old twins Tom and Andy Craft arrive in the region as raw recruits in the 106th Infantry Division. They, along with Army intelligence and the rest of the Allied forces, believe that the Germans have been permanently routed since the Normandy invasion of June 1944. However, the Germans launch a quarter of a million soldiers into thin Allied lines. Tom and Andy are separated, communication lines are broken, and command is confused in the first days of the battle.

FRANK BONHAM (1914–   )
War Beneath the Sea (1962; 253 PAGES; M/M)

Keith Stocker is on his way from Honolulu to San Francisco in early 1942 when the freighter he is on is sunk by a Japanese torpedo. After being rescued by a submarine, Keith develops an interest in subs. He enlists in the Navy and attends submarine school in Connecticut. The rest of the novel follows him throughout World War II in the submarine service. He becomes an expert sonarman and an integral part of an expert crew. The sub plies the Pacific and engages in action near Guadalcanal, the Coral Sea, and the Solomon Islands; it also spends stretches of time in Pearl Harbor, Australia, and San Francisco. The novel includes a glossary of naval and submarine terms.

HAL BORLAND (1900–1978)
When the Legends Die (1963; ABOUT 213 PAGES; M/M)

The story of a boy's search for identity, this novel is set in Colorado and other parts of the West in 1910. The family of Thomas Black Bull, a young American Indian boy, has made an effort to fit into reservation life, but their attempt does not work. Tom and his mother and father flee from the Ute Indian Reservation after Tom's father kills a man. In the mountains, Tom's parents teach him how to survive in the traditional Native American ways. Both parents die, and Tom is brought to a reservation school, where he suffers physical and mental abuse. Leaving the reservation with a small-time rodeo rider, he spends some time learning to ride. Finally, Tom returns to his life in the mountains. The novel is a searing criticism of the methods used on Indian reservations to make Native Americans adapt to modern life. Whether intentional or not, the novel also presents an unsettling look at the cruel treatment of horses in rodeos.

JOHN BRICK (1922–1973)
Captives of the Senecas (1964; 146 PAGES; E/E)

Steve Corwin and Jack Berckly are in the 12th Pennsylvania Regiment during the American Revolution. In 1778, during a lull in Revolutionary War activity, they decide to leave camp on the Susquehanna River to hunt deer. Suddenly, they are surrounded and captured by Seneca Indians, who take them to their base camp at Catherine's Town (near Seneca Lake in New York). Among other prisoners is Sally White. All three settle in to wait out the winter and take a chance to escape. During this time, they observe and learn to appreciate the Indian culture. They also learn about the politics of the Indian Six Nations, the Indian-British alliance, and the approach of colonial general John Sullivan's army. The story climaxes with an escape attempt down the Chemung River in southern New York.

CAROL RYRIE BRINK (1895–1981)
Caddie Woodlawn (1935; ABOUT 270 PAGES; M/M)

At the time this novel was written, in 1935, the real Caddie Woodlawn was eighty-two years old. Her memories of a pioneer childhood spent in western Wisconsin in the 1860's and 1870's form the basis of the story. The free-spirited Caddie's life revolves from one season to another; thus experiences such as planting, harvesting, winter, and schooldays work their way through the plot. Despite the presence of civilization and "law and order," there is an undercurrent of American Indian threat throughout. Caddie, however, believes in living peacefully with the Indians.

DEE BROWN (1908–)
Killdeer Mountain (1983; 279 PAGES; M/M)

This unusual story centers around frontier life and an 1864 American Indian battle. Journalist Sam Morrison is searching for an interesting piece for the *Saint Louis Herald*. From a dock on the Missouri River in 1866, Morrison boards a steamer upriver. On board, he learns about Charles Rawley, an Ohio senator's son, who became both a coward and a hero at the Killdeer Mountain battle in the Dakota Territory. The journalist, realizing he has a compelling but conflicting story of Rawley's behavior in the Indian battle, sets out to investigate the mystery by interviewing the characters involved. The device of untangling a mystery within a tale of frontier life makes for effective characters and storytelling.

ROBERT BURCH (1925–)
Hut School and the Wartime Home-Front Heroes (1974; 129 PAGES; E/E)

Life on the U.S. home front during World War II has not received much serious interest until the last decade or so. Thus, this novel, which tells of young people's adjustment to war, is a good contribution. Kate Coleman and her family live in Georgia; for a time they think of the war as an inconvenience. Then, Kate's school becomes overcrowded and can no longer hold all of its students. Kate and her friends begin to attend school in an old cabin. This experience, plus news of relatives in far-off places, deaths of friends and relatives, and shortages, eventually teach the children what World War II means.

PETER BURCHARD (1921–)
North by Night (1962; 178 PAGES; E/E)

Union Army Lieutenants Bradford and Kelly are part of the 7th Connecticut Volunteers located on islands off the shore of the Carolinas early in the Civil War. Their mission is to establish a base of operations against Charleston, South Carolina, a major Confederate city. In a charge against a key fort, the men are captured and put into a Confederate prison. The story of this imprisonment, the prisoners' relationship with a Confederate captain, their escape, and their journey back to Union lines is the major focus of the book. (Lieutenant Bradford, one of the main characters of this novel, is based on an actual person related to the author.)

EUGENE BURDICK (1918–1965) AND HARVEY WHEELER (1918–)
Fail-Safe (1962; ABOUT 116 PAGES; M/M)

Although dated, this story still provides a good account of tensions and the possible result of these tensions between two superpowers—the U.S. and the U.S.S.R. An accidental incident takes U.S. bombers into the Soviet Union to bomb Moscow. The action takes place within a few hours and involves the Strategic Air Command in Omaha, Nebraska, the president in Washington, D.C., and the Soviet premier in the U.S.S.R. Other characters are the U.S. Russian translator in the War Room in the White House, the U.S. ambassador to the U.S.S.R. in Moscow, and the Soviet ambassador to the United Nations in New York. There are some technical inaccuracies in the description of how the U.S.–U.S.S.R. emergency open-line operated.

W.E. BUTTERWORTH (1929–   )
Orders to Vietnam (1968; 159 PAGES; E/E)

One of the technological advances in the Vietnam War was the extensive use of helicopters in combat operations. Written before the full bitterness of Vietnam settled in, this novel chronicles the training and combat experiences of Bill Byrnes as a helicopter pilot stationed at Pleiku, Vietnam. Bill has been drafted for a two-year hitch after dropping out of West Point in less than two months and attending college for less than a year. His father is a career army officer stationed in Vietnam. During his time in Vietnam, Bill must get used to steamy weather, good men who die, incompetent officers, and the death of a close friend. On a rest-and-recreation trip to Honolulu, he also must learn to deal with his father.

TAYLOR CALDWELL (1900–1985)
Captains and the Kings (1972; 637 PAGES; D/D)

This novel explores the possibility of a powerful, nefarious worldwide government. Irish immigrant Joseph Armagh is twelve years old when he arrives in America in the early 1850's. Mistreated by the Americans as he was by the English, Joe disdains allegiance to any country or people. Over the years, he ruthlessly accumulates a vast fortune and political power. Becoming a force within the international money and power brokers known as the Invisible Government, he and they manipulate governments and businesses worldwide—even participating in the assassinations of Presidents Lincoln and McKinley. Joe threatens to destroy an honest politician, who kills himself—but first puts a curse on the Armagh family. The Armaghs are stricken with repeated tragedies as years go by. Joe supports his son Rory to run for president of the United States. Rory makes the lethal mistake of divulging to Joe his intent to expose the Invisible Government to the American voters.

BEBE MOORE CAMPBELL (1950–   )
Your Blues Ain't Like Mine (1992; 332 PAGES; D/D)

This story takes place in 1950's Mississippi, when the Supreme Court ruling on school integration resulted in political, social, and personal upheaval. A young African-American man is murdered by a cowardly white man who wants to please his violent, bigoted father. The Honorable Men of Hopewell, Mississippi—a group of farmers and businessmen who are the behind-the-scenes power of the rural town—decide to allow a mock trial. Their decision is prompted by the presence of national news media investigating the murder. The white man is found not guilty, setting in motion a black backlash that affects the social and economic backbone of the town. By the 1980's, integration has permeated the town while racist attitudes continue on both sides. This is a gripping account of a tumultuous time in American history and a thorough examination of black-white relations. Sexual situations are presented.

NATALIE SAVAGE CARLSON (1906–)
The Empty Schoolhouse (1965; 119 PAGES; E/E)

In a slight twist on a 1960's desegregation story, *The Empty Schoolhouse* tells of the attempt to desegregate a parochial school in French Grove, Louisiana. Ten-year-old Lullah Royall, a black girl, and Oralee Fleury, a white girl, are best friends. They go to the same church, where blacks sit in the back, but they do not go to the same school. When the bishop announces that all children will be welcomed at St. Joseph's school, Lullah cannot wait to attend with her friend. The following chain of events includes threats against black families, attacks against black homes, and a "white flight" out of St. Joseph's school. Lullah's determined attempts to go to school and keep her friend, along with the fact that she is shot, bring the town residents to important conclusions.

NATALIE SAVAGE CARLSON (1906–)
Marchers for the Dream (1969; 127 PAGES; E/E)

This story is told from the perspective of an eleven-year-old African-American girl in the late 1960's. The action occurs after Martin Luther King's death in 1968 and at the time of Resurrection City in Washington, D.C. Bethany Jackson's immediate concern is that her home in Massachusetts is about to be bulldozed in a spurt of urban renewal. The Jackson family is split on what actions to take to resolve their problem of finding housing—an area where discrimination is practiced despite the law forbidding it. Bethany accompanies her spirited great-grandmother to Resurrection City, and there they find hope and a possible solution to their problem.

FORREST CARTER (1927?–1979)
The Education of Little Tree (1977; 216 PAGES; E/E)

In the 1930's, in rural Tennessee, a five-year-old orphan is given to his grandparents to be raised. Granpa is half Cherokee, Granma is full blood; they name the boy Little Tree. Over the next five years, living with his grandparents in their hillside cabin, Little Tree learns how to live with the land, and how to love. He survives a period in an orphanage, then returns happily to the mountainside. His grandfather teaches him how to make whiskey; both grandparents share with him the ways of his people. Finally, Little Tree has to learn how to accept grief, and to build his own life while remaining faithful to the trust his grandparents gave him. After publication, *The Education of Little Tree* was widely acclaimed, described by reviewers as "poignant, happy, warm, and filled with love and respect for the Indian way of life." Admirers of the book were shocked in 1991 when Carter's widow confirmed rumors that he was actually Asa Carter, a prominent white supremacist in the 1950's and 1960's. Is *Little Tree* a memoir of Carter's youth, or is it a work of fiction? We'll probably never know. But after Mrs. Carter's revelation the book went on to become a fiction best-seller, and is still hailed as a children's classic.

WILLA CATHER (1873–1947)
My Ántonia (1918; ABOUT 368 PAGES; M/M)

Cather's classic story describes pioneer life in Nebraska in the late nineteenth century. The story is told from the point of view of Jim Burden, who is about ten when he starts his recollections. Jim is an orphan who comes to live with his grandparents near Black Hawk. One group of neighbors is the Shimerda family, the first Bohemians in the neighborhood. Ántonia Shimerda, who is about fourteen when Jim meets her, impresses Jim from that time on. She struggles to learn English and helps her family on the farm. When Ántonia's father dies, she hires herself out to various families. After one unhappy affair that produces a child, Ántonia marries a Bohemian. Together, they raise a dozen children and make a successful life on the prairie.

WILLA CATHER (1873–1947)
One of Ours (1922; ABOUT 459 PAGES; D/D)

This narrative is divided into three sections. Claude Wheeler is a sensitive, shy young man living on a Nebraska farm in 1914 in the months before World War I begins in Europe. In the first section, Claude is at college and at the farm, following the rhythm of the seasons. He interacts with the first native-born generation of immigrants, including Swedes, Danes, Germans, and Bohemians. The second section follows Claude as he suffers through a bad marriage to Enid, who is overcome by missionary zeal and eventually goes to China. In the last section, Claude enlists in the army and goes to fight in France. Cather won a Pulitzer Prize for this novel.

WILLA CATHER (1873–1947)
O Pioneers! (1913; ABOUT 306 PAGES; M/M)

The Bergsons, shipbuilders from Norway, come to the Nebraska prairie in the 1880's to grow wheat and corn on land that had always sprouted grass and wildflowers. The elder Mr. Bergson dies, and his daughter Alexandra runs the farm. At this time it is rare for a daughter to assume farming responsibilities when adult sons are available. Over time, Alexandra develops a deep, almost obsessive love for the land. This love is matched by her love for her brother Emil. Alexandra eventually achieves success with the farm and sends Emil off to receive a university education. However, Alexandra's success breeds jealousy from her other brothers.

EDNA WALKER CHANDLER (1908–1982)
Indian Paintbrush (1975; 119 PAGES; E/E)

A plea for bilingualism and multiculturalism is at the heart of this contemporary story. Young Maria Lopez is half Mexican and half Sioux. She speaks Spanish and English, but not Sioux. After her Mexican father's death, it becomes necessary for Maria and her mother and brothers to move back to South Dakota and the Sioux relatives. Because of her "half-caste" background, Maria feels that she does not fit in. In addition, older brother Pedro works on a dam project, which upsets older Indians who feel the environment will be ruined. Into this picture steps Jean Brave, the new teacher. She combines characteristics of all three societies—white, Mexican, and Sioux—and she speaks English, Spanish, and Sioux.

BARBARA CHASE-RIBOUD (1939–   )
Sally Hemings (1979; 344 PAGES; M/M)

The lives of two families, the black Hemings and the white Jeffersons, are detailed within this narrative set against colonial America and the institution of slavery. Sally Hemings is a young slave belonging to Thomas Jefferson. She is also half-sister to Jefferson's deceased wife, Martha. In 1787, Sally accompanies Jefferson's daughter Polly to Paris, where Jefferson is serving as ambassador to France. While in Paris, the fifteen-year-old slave becomes mistress to Jefferson, then forty-three. The sensitive, intelligent, and beautiful Sally can remain in France and be free. Instead, she returns to Monticello, Virginia, with Jefferson—on his false promise that she and any children borne of their union will be free. Like her mother before her, Sally kept her own family name of Hemings, but she lived her life for the pleasure of the white slaveholder. Sally never left Monticello. This novel chronicles sixty years of American social and political history.

K. FOLLIS CHEATHAM (1943–   )
Bring Home the Ghost (1980; 279 PAGES; M/M)

In the nineteenth century, deep friendships between blacks and whites were rare due to lack of social contact and persistent racial tension. *Bring Home the Ghost* tells the story of the relationship of two Alabama boys between 1827 and 1836. Tolin Cobb, white son of a plantation owner, and Jason, one of the slaves, form a bond after Jason saves Tolin's life. Eventually, they leave the plantation after Creek Indian attacks and head west to certain—if unsettling—adventures. Their journeys take them through Wyoming, Missouri, and Oklahoma, with the intent of reaching Oregon. The author has researched to find details of African-American people's lives at that time. Also authentically described are frontier activities as well as various Indian tribes' attitudes and restrictions concerning African Americans.

KATE CHOPIN (1851–1904)
The Awakening (1899; ABOUT 109 PAGES; D/D)

Twenty-eight-year-old Edna Pontellier is an attractive, well-to-do, and well-bred woman of late-nineteenth-century Louisiana. Her husband is considered nearly perfect by conventional standards, and they have two fine children. Yet Edna is vaguely unhappy and feels strangely out of place in a society in which she was born to excel. Unfortunately, personal freedom and independence are not acceptable qualities in Edna's time. Yearning for the personal freedom society condemns in women, Edna desires a life she cannot have—and as a woman, "should not" want. Trying to sever the ties that bind her to husband and children, Edna pursues a painting career and a home of her own. Finding she does not have the strength to fight the strong bonds that society holds women to, she succumbs to a tragic end.

PATRICIA CLAPP (1912–)
Constance: A Story of Early Plymouth (1968; 244 PAGES; M/M)

Using the device of a journal, *Constance* develops the life of Constance Hopkins, an original settler in Plymouth, Massachusetts. The book cover the years 1620–1626, from the time Constance is fourteen until she marries at age twenty. During these six years, half of the settlers die early from illness, and new settlers arrive in Massachusetts from England. They bring new life to the colony—but also bring unscrupulous men who sow seeds of disunity. Indians prove to be both a puzzlement and a problem, as some welcome the settlers and some do not, while the colonists try to understand Native-American ways. Complex and life-threatening situations exist side by side with details of the everyday life of Constance and others in the colony. (Constance Hopkins was an ancestor of the author.)

PATRICIA CLAPP (1912–)
I'm Deborah Sampson (1978; 167 PAGES; E/E)

This is a novelization of the life of Deborah Sampson, who actually served in the American army as a man. In 1783, Private Robert Shurtlieff leaves the Continental Army of the newly free America. Shurtlieff is commended for bravery and good conduct while a soldier. In reality, the young soldier is Deborah Sampson, who has disguised herself as a man and served in the army undetected. The author has Deborah tell this remarkable tale of her harsh early life as a half-orphan, her decision to join the army, her failure at her first attempt to enlist, and her success on the second attempt. Service in the army surrounded by an all-male population is the main focus, but Deborah also tells what happens to her after her adventure.

ANN NOLAN CLARK (1896–)
All This Wild Land (1976; 177 PAGES; E/E)

Immigrants to America often settled in areas that resembled the home they left. This was true of many Scandinavians who came to the northern Midwest. This story concerns the lives of eleven-year-old Maiju and her family, who come to Minnesota from Finland in 1876. The town of Yankee Mill is hardly more than mud streets and a few wooden structures. After months of travel and work, Maiju and her family have a house, a sauna, and a crop. The crop is destroyed by hail, and Maiju's father goes to town to earn money. Maiju and her mother remain behind to endure the harsh Minnesota winter and to learn the lessons of hard work and courage taught all immigrants to America.

ELIZABETH COATSWORTH (1893–1986)
Here I Stay (1938; ABOUT 243 PAGES; M/M)

Margaret Winslow makes an important decision when she decides to stay in her Maine settlement rather than move with neighbors and family members to the Ohio country in 1817. She is the only one who remains. Despite a succession of heavy winters and the death of her father, she feels deeply attached to the land they have cleared and the home they have built together. After the neighbors leave, life is still eventful as one season follows another. There are Indian visitors, Vermont travelers, rounds of plowing and harvesting, and milking and sewing. In the end, Margaret has no reason to regret her decision.

ELIZABETH COATSWORTH (1893–1986)
Sword of the Wilderness (1936; ABOUT 156 PAGES; E/E)

Maine in the late 1600's was a land of temporary fishing settlements slowly evolving into a small number of permanent towns. Because of unsettled boundaries, disputed land claims, and land that ran into Canada, there were many disputes among the French, the English settlers, and the local Indians. In addition, France and England were at war. In this setting, Seth Hubbard is out on his daily farm errands when he is attacked by Indians and taken captive. He endures the gauntlet, constant moves, and a harsh winter. He meets other captives: John Hammond and Keoka, a girl brought up by the Indians. Eventually, Seth returns to his Maine home after an exchange of captives takes place in Quebec.

JAMES LINCOLN COLLIER (1928–) AND CHRISTOPHER COLLIER (1930–)
The Clock (1992; 159 PAGES; E/M)

The Clock questions the value of progress when it means losing control of one's own time and life. In 1810, a small town in Connecticut has become economically dependent on a wool mill. Fifteen-year-old Annie Steele wants to become a schoolteacher, but is forced into millwork to pay off her father's debts. Annie's mother is sympathetic but dares not challenge her husband's irrational financial decisions. The latest is the purchase of an expensive factory-made clock on credit. In addition to forcing Annie into giving up her plans, the clock changes her farm family's lives dramatically. Now they are governed by her father's clock instead of the familiar guides of sunrise and sunset, weather, seasons, and bodily needs. At the mill, Annie hates the brutal, rigidly enforced efficiency methods and the overseer who sexually harasses her. Her father belittles her concerns and will not let her quit because he needs her income. Annie has lost control over her life both at home and at the despised mill, but refuses to give up her dreams.

JAMES LINCOLN COLLIER (1928–) AND CHRISTOPHER COLLIER (1930–)
Jump Ship to Freedom (1981; 198 PAGES; E/E)

In 1787, Daniel Arabus and his widowed mother are slaves to ship's Captain Ivers and Mrs. Ivers of Stratford, Connecticut. Captain Ivers has stolen $600 from Daniel and his mother. Daniel takes the money back and carries it aboard Captain Ivers' ship, intending to buy his and his mother's freedom. After the ship arrives in New York Harbor for repairs, Daniel jumps ship and finds his way to Black Sam's Fraunces' Tavern. Daniel meets an antislavery Quaker, who sends him to deliver an important message regarding how the slavery issue should be dealt with in the Constitution. In so doing, Daniel meets General Washington and Alexander Hamilton—and secures his and his mother's freedom at last. Some of the novel's dialogue is nonstandard English.

JAMES LINCOLN COLLIER (1928–) AND CHRISTOPHER COLLIER (1930–)
My Brother Sam Is Dead (1974; 245 PAGES; M/M)

This story takes place in Redding, Connecticut (near New Haven) during the Revolutionary War. Tim, the youngest son in the Meeker family, tells about his family's divided loyalties during the war. His brother Sam, age sixteen, runs off to join the colonists against the British. His father and the rest of the family, who run a tavern and raise cattle, live in what is considered to be a Tory town whose citizens are on the British side. Tim describes the conflict between his father—who is mostly against the war but also has sympathies for the British—and his brother Sam—who fights for three years on the colonists' side. In an ironic twist, the colonial army, with which Sam has fought loyally, wrongly convicts Sam of being a cattle thief.

JAMES LINCOLN COLLIER (1928–) AND CHRISTOPHER COLLIER (1930–)
The Winter Hero (1978; 152 PAGES; E/E)

Shay's Rebellion is a little-known incident in early American history. However, it was very significant because this rebellion reflected two conditions of the country between 1775 and 1789. First, there was no federal constitution in effect; second, the states had considerable powers over taxation and commerce. The story is told from the youth Justin Conkey's viewpoint in 1787. In Massachusetts, Justin's brother-in-law Peter and many others are weighed down with excessive taxation. Peter joins an "army" called Shay's Regulators, who oppose what they consider tyrannical behavior by tax collectors and the state government. Young Justin acts as a spy, participates in the fighting, and sees that there will be a new government.

HILA COLMAN
Ellie's Inheritance (1979; 181 PAGES; E/M)

Complex events and attitudes surround this story of a young Jewish girl in New York City, whose family becomes poor during the Depression years of the 1930's. Ellie Levine tells about her life as she seeks work successively in an office, in an anti-Fascist (anti-German) organization, and in the fashion world. She struggles with the problems of class and religious prejudice against a background of the political developments of socialism and Nazism in Europe. The simple story line is deceptive; it includes a considerable amount of the history and politics of the 1930's.

JAMES FENIMORE COOPER (1789–1851)
The Deerslayer (1841; ABOUT 567 PAGES; D/D)

This is the first of *The Leatherstocking Tales* in the order of events within the novel series. However, it was actually the last of the tales to be published, which can lead to interesting discussions of how Cooper handled his characters. Natty Bumppo is introduced here as a young man just reaching maturity and independence. (In the five *Leatherstocking Tales,* Natty Bumppo is also identified variously as the Deerslayer, Pathfinder, Leatherstocking, and Hawkeye.) In this novel Natty is the Deerslayer, but he has yet to kill a man. The story is set in New York State on Lake Otsego prior to 1760. Natty's companion is the Indian Chingachgook. Together, they begin on the path to becoming warriors in their frontier society. By the close of the novel, Natty has become an accomplished man of the forest.

JAMES FENIMORE COOPER (1789–1851)
The Last of the Mohicans (1826; ABOUT 404 PAGES; D/D)

Part of the series of *The Leatherstocking Tales, The Last of the Mohicans* begins in 1757. It is the second year of the French and Indian Wars—battles between France and England over supremacy on the North American continent. After a massacre at Fort William Henry in New York by the Indian allies of French General Montcalm, two women—Alice and Cora—are captured by the enemy Hurons. Natty Bumppo (called Hawkeye in this book) and his Indian companions seek the Hurons and their hostages in the forest. This novel can be read on several levels: as an action yarn, as a tale of the near-extinction of the Native Americans in eastern North America, as an exploration of nature and civilization, and as a racial comment.

JAMES FENIMORE COOPER (1789–1851)
The Pathfinder (1840; ABOUT 499 PAGES; D/D)

The third in the order of events of Natty Bumppo's life in *The Leatherstocking Tales, The Pathfinder* concerns the forest warrior in the midst of the French and Indian Wars (1756–1763). He is still a young man, but well established in his reputation as a scout and marksman, guiding parties of travelers westward from New York. He encounters dangers from the French, the Indians, and the British. He also must struggle against the physical hardships of traveling through the wilderness and on the Great Lakes. Natty Bumppo is accompanied by a Mohican Indian friend. During the course of the story, Natty falls in love for the first and only time in the series.

JAMES FENIMORE COOPER (1789–1851)
The Pioneers (1823; ABOUT 477 PAGES; D/D)

Natty Bumppo is seventy-one years old when he is introduced in this novel. Chronologically, it is the fourth book of *The Leatherstocking Tales,* although it was actually the first book that Cooper wrote about this character. Cooper writes about a most familiar area—that of Lake Otsego, New York, in 1793 (seven years after the author's own father founded the original settlement of Cooperstown). Bumppo is a disillusioned man, living among the group of pioneers who become identified with the woods, the water, and the wildlife. Another group of pioneers who follow intend to tame the wilderness with ax and rifle. The relation between these two pioneer groups, Bumppo's role, and the setting itself are the main themes of the work.

JAMES FENIMORE COOPER (1789–1851)
The Prairie (1827; ABOUT 453 PAGES; D/D)

This is the last of the five *Leatherstocking Tales,* which cover the life of frontiersman Natty Bumppo from the French and Indian Wars period until the early nineteenth century. The scene is west of the Rocky Mountains in about 1804, or shortly after the Louisiana Purchase. The barrier of the Rocky Mountains plus the relatively dry land make the area difficult to settle. (When Cooper wrote the story, the territory was barely occupied.) Natty Bumppo is now a trapper. He has been driven out of his beloved forests and is not physically able to carry out his hunting and scouting activities. However, he experiences a capture by hostile Indians, a buffalo stampede, and a prairie fire. Bumppo dies peacefully at the end.

STEPHEN CRANE (1871–1900)
The Red Badge of Courage (1895; ABOUT 180 PAGES; M/M)

Crane produced one of the great war novels of any war or country in the story of the boy Henry Fleming and his experiences in the U.S. Civil War (1861–1865). Fleming's story unfolds through five phases: a period before battle, his first battle, his second battle and flight, his wanderings behind the lines, and his return to battle. The major theme of the novel is the initiation of a boy into manhood, in this case through the experiences of war. However, Fleming learns first that war is not heroic in the way in which he has dreamed. Second, to become a man, society has defined that he must abandon his self in order to fight courageously as part of the group. Third, he must hope to be wounded, to win a "red badge of courage," to be accepted as a man.

ANNE ELIOT CROMPTON (1930–)
The Ice Trail (1980; 89 PAGES; E/E)

According to a New Hampshire legend, Abenaki Indians on the north shore of Lake Champlain captured a white boy named Daniel Abbott in 1703 and kept him for five years. *The Ice Trail* is based on that legend. When braves return from a raid with ice skates but without Daniel's Indian foster father, Daniel—now Tanial—plots to escape using the ice skates. Helped by his foster brother, Molsemis, Tanial begins his winter journey back to his home and the dim but persistent memory of the white world. Told primarily from the Indian point of view, the story provides insight into early-eighteenth-century Native American life in eastern North America and the problems of survival in a harsh environment.

BETTY SUE CUMMINGS (1948–)
Now, Ameriky (1979; 172 PAGES; E/E)

In the mid-nineteenth century, Brigid Clery, the oldest of the Clery children, flees Ireland's great famine. The famine not only has killed many but also forced thousands to emigrate to America. Brigid wants to sail to America, too. She hopes to find work there and raise passage money for the rest of the family and her fiancé, Padraic. Many of the hardships suffered by immigrants are seen through Brigid's experiences. She must walk from her village to Dublin, then sail from Dublin to Liverpool. The long, severe journey from Liverpool is a nightmare for a young woman with no protection. However, when Brigid lands in New York City, she still must experience the realities of slum living in the Irish section. Finally, she must decide what to do about her future with Padraic and whether or not to move west.

CYNTHIA DEFELICE
Weasel (1990; 119 PAGES; E/E)

By 1839, the U.S. Congress and the state of Ohio have removed most Native Americans from the area along the Ohio River. Twelve-year-old Nathan Fowler and his younger sister, Molly, live on a small farm along the river with their widowed father—taking advantage of cheap, unsettled land. When their father fails to return from a hunting trip, the children set off with Ezra, a mute woodsman, to find him. Ezra cannot speak because his tongue has been cut out by a man the Indians call Weasel, a murderous former Indian fighter who had once been sent out by the government to drive Indians from Ohio. Now Weasel kills settlers and animals for sport. Nathan finds his father cruelly injured by Weasel, and vows revenge. His father explains that revenge and hatred rob people of the joys of everyday life and that killing does not make a man. Defying his father, Nathan sneaks off to kill Weasel, only to find that he is already dead. Nathan learns valuable lessons about Indian life, the uselessness of hatred, and the futility of revenge.

JOHN DOS PASSOS (1896–1970)
Three Soldiers (1921; ABOUT 471 PAGES; M/D)

Dos Passos tells the stories of three soldiers, from different states and backgrounds, who enter the armed services during World War I. He contrasts the attitudes of young men seeking to find careers and glory and those who find both service life and the prospect of war dehumanizing and totally without just cause. Dos Passos examines the worth of human life versus the often unknown reasons for war, and finally questions the need for taking any human life. All three soldiers, entering the service for different reasons, find disappointment and life-shattering experiences to be the result of fighting for a cause they have never truly understood. The novel contains sexist language and sexual themes in moderation and explores ethnic differences.

THEODORE DREISER (1871–1945)
An American Tragedy (1925; ABOUT 844 PAGES; D/D)

An American Tragedy takes place in the 1920's—the glory days of capitalism and industrialism. This era made some people fabulously rich and passed others by completely, establishing marked differences in social and economic classes and opportunities. Clyde Griffiths is a poor, uneducated son of drifting evangelist missionaries. Clyde resents his circumstances and looks for a way out, starting as a bellhop in a luxurious hotel in Missouri when he is sixteen. Moving to Chicago, Clyde is working in a businessmen's club when he meets his rich uncle from New York. Uncle Samuel Griffiths opens a door of wonderful opportunity for Clyde. However, a promising career is shattered when Clyde, hoping to marry a wealthy socialite, murders a girl of low social status with whom he has had an affair. *An American Tragedy* is a commentary on the promises and pitfalls of instant wealth, the effects of poverty and lack of education, and the politics of social status in America.

ALLEN DRURY (1918–   )
Advise and Consent (1959; 613 PAGES; D/D)

This is the first in a four-book saga. One of Drury's goals in writing *Advise and Consent* was to comment on the politics of the time the novel was written (the late 1950's). With the passing of time, the novel has taken on historical interest as a comment on a prior generation of Washington politicians. The book is organized into four major segments titled by the main character; each segment could almost stand alone. Together, they form a complex story of what happens when the president asks the Senate to "advise and consent" to his controversial nominee for secretary of state. Into the story comes a wily older senator, a demagogue with a smear campaign, a presidential hopeful who will not sacrifice his principles, and the candidate himself—qualified but destined not to be confirmed. Drury won the Pulitzer Prize for this work.

ALLEN DRURY (1918–   )
A Shade of Difference (1962; 677 PAGES; D/D)

In *A Shade of Difference* Drury continues with some of the characters from *Advise and Consent,* placing them with new characters in the setting of the United Nations in the 1960's. The central problem is the desire for independence of a British colony, Gorotoland, and how the various delegates to the U.N. react to this. This problem has effects in the U.S. because of the civil rights movement; a black congressman plays a major role as events occur. In addition, the impact on the presidency and the Congress is examined. How other countries—especially the Soviet Union, Panama, and some neutral countries—play upon the Gorotoland and U.S. civil rights situations becomes a theme.

ALLEN DRURY (1918–   )
Capable of Honor (1966; 528 PAGES; D/D)

In *Capable of Honor* Drury carries forward many of the characters from *Advise and Consent* and *A Shade of Difference*. His focus is the influence of the media—press, radio, and TV—in the 1960's. Walter Dobius is a famous Washington columnist who is influential among his colleagues. With Dobius at the center, Drury explores how two major international crises—a rebellion in the African nation of Gorotoland (a British colony) and a problem in Panama—affect the media, domestic politics, and foreign affairs. Drury raises the question of how much and how purposefully the media control or interfere with world and domestic events.

ALLEN DRURY (1918–   )
Preserve and Protect (1968; 391 PAGES; D/D)

With *Preserve and Protect,* Drury closes his four-book saga of 1960's American political life in Washington and at the United Nations. Just after his renomination as party candidate, President Harley Hudson dies under mysterious circumstances. This leaves the party without a standard-bearer and no organized way to select one. The results of this central event, along with other domestic and international crises, lead to considerable violence within the United States. The war in the British colony of Gorotoland grows larger in efforts to win independence, and anti-American feeling in Panama threatens to explode in a dangerous plot. While this book was being prepared for publication, Robert Kennedy and Martin Luther King, Jr., were killed.

WALTER D. EDMONDS (1903–   )
Drums Along the Mohawk (1936; ABOUT 466 PAGES; D/D)

When 1776 brings rumblings of war even to the remote wilderness of the Mohawk Valley in New York, newlyweds Gil and Lana Martin have more immediate concerns. They are clearing the new land and planting crops. Before long, however, the war rages up and down the valley. The Indian allies of the British cut a path of destruction by looting, burning, kidnapping, and mutilating most of what is in their path. The Martins and others in the valley combine to fight the Indians. They also have to fight a still-inexperienced Continental Congress, which ignores pleas for relief. Outnumbered by trained British troops and the Indians, the settlers battle to win the valley for the American side.

Walter D. Edmonds (1903–)
The Matchlock Gun (1941; 50 pages; e/e)

Though still very popular, this children's novel reflects a narrow, stereotypical view of Native Americans. In 1757, Edward Van Alstyne is ten years old when his mother, Gertrude, shows him how to use an outdated matchlock gun. His father, Captain Teunis Van Alstyne, has kept the gun because it is a family heirloom, but he feels it is really not very useful. The matchlock gun certainly is of use when Edward's father is away, and Indians attack the family in their Hudson Valley, New York, homestead. Although neither Edward nor his mother knows much about it, they rig the gun up to a window. When the Indians attack, the huge old gun saves Edward, his little sister, his mother, and their farm.

Sally Edwards (1929–)
George Midgett's War (1985; 135 pages; e/e)

The fishermen of Okracoke, on the outer banks of North Carolina, want no involvement in the American Revolutionary War against the British. It is not their war, for they have gone about their business untouched—until a beloved old lady is murdered by the British. Enraged, the islanders undertake a daring mission to deliver supplies to George Washington's forces at Valley Forge. Fourteen-year-old George Midgett and his father take the lead in the effort. Rich in historical and social commentary on the barrier islands, this novel chronicles not only the islanders' war efforts, but a highly believable account of the survivors of Roanoke Island. According to this story, the Roanoke inhabitants (English and Indian) scattered after a storm, and some migrated to the North Carolina outer banks.

Ralph Ellison (1914–)
Invisible Man (1952; 496 pages; d/d)

A novel with tremendous influence on both black and white society, *Invisible Man* traces the life of an intense young African-American man, beginning with his high school graduation between World Wars I and II. He attends a black college in the South, but because of a bizarre incident with a white trustee, he is expelled. He then moves north and takes on a nightmarish job in a paint factory. He becomes involved with the "Brotherhood" in New York's Harlem and finally is embroiled in a race riot. Along this route, the man learns what being black—being invisible—means; he reaches a startling conclusion as to how to live in this society.

ELOISE ENGLE (1923–)
Dawn Mission: A Flight Nurse in Korea (1962; 176 PAGES; E/E)

Until recent changes in military regulations to conform with antidiscrimination legislation, women in the service only achieved the higher ranks (including general) in all-female units—principally nursing corps. Female nurses have served in all combat areas where men have fought. This novel focuses on flight nurses in the Korean War. Jill Saunders, daughter of well-known parents, is the heroine. Jill serves on mercy missions which pick up wounded soldiers and deliver them to hospitals in Japan. Serving with her are a medical technician, a World War II veteran flight nurse, an air-evacuation copilot, and a newspaperwoman interested in a good story.

NORMA FARBER (1909–1984)
Mercy Short (1982; 135 PAGES; M/M)

This story, in journal format, is based on an account of the real Mercy Short written by Boston clergyman Cotton Mather (1663–1728). Mercy Short is an indentured servant who is captured by Indians and suffers the murder of her family by the Tawney tribe. Now ransomed and freed by the Boston church of Cotton Mather, Mercy sets down her experiences in a journal from 1692 to 1693. She writes at the direction of Mather, who seeks to exorcise, or free, her from her "bedevilment." Mather has established a reputation as an exorcist during the Salem witch trials of 1692, and in the following winter, he is sure he can free Mercy Short.

JAMES T. FARRELL (1904–1979)
Studs Lonigan: A Trilogy (1935; ABOUT 465 PAGES; D/D)

Interwoven into this story is a discussion of American values and morals, national politics, economic policies, and working-class strife. Studs Lonigan grows up in an Irish neighborhood on the East Coast between the World Wars. His father is a poorly educated but moderately successful painting contractor, who wants Studs to get an education and take over the business. Studs prefers to hang out and drink with his friends rather than work. Raw bootleg liquor is all that is available because of Prohibition laws. After several of his friends die from the effects of liquor, Studs drinks more moderately—but too late to prevent heart disease. Worried about his health and the aimlessness of his life, Studs searches for work that will not strain his heart. Even though the stock market collapses and the Great Depression begins, Studs determines to be responsible and marries his pregnant girlfriend. But Studs contracts pneumonia and dies at age thirty. The novel contains sexual situations and frank language.

HOWARD FAST (1914–   )
April Morning (1961; 199 PAGES; E/E)

This story unfolds during a thirty-six-hour period covering the day before and the day of the initial battle of the American Revolution. Adam Cooper is fifteen years old when the Revolutionary War begins in April 1775 in his hometown of Lexington, Massachusetts. Adam has a prickly relationship with his father and complex relationships with his brother, mother, grandmother, and a neighbor girl. The excellent dialogue among the characters reveals that Adam's father is a Committee of Correspondence member, that Adam is about to grow out of his boyhood, and that he will experience being under fire from the British.

HOWARD FAST (1914–   )
Freedom Road (1944; 261 PAGES; M/M)

In a brief period after the Civil War, when African-American men have been given freedom and equality, Gideon Jackson becomes a landowner and statesman in the deep South. Working with other freed slaves and poor whites, Jackson takes over an abandoned plantation. Later, he educates himself and becomes a state representative. Before freedom and equality can take root, however, the Ku Klux Klan comes to power. Active in lynchings, burning of homes, rapes, and slaughter, the Klan destroys all that Jackson has worked to create. Ultimately, black Americans are stripped of the legal equality that has briefly been theirs. Jackson dies defending his black and white friends and their lands.

HOWARD FAST (1914–   )
The Immigrants (1977; 386 PAGES; M/M)

In 1888, Italian immigrants Anna and Joseph Lavette, like millions of others, come to America by ship. *The Immigrants* (first in a series of novels about the Lavette family) is the saga of their immigration and life in their new country. The story describes Joseph's work on the railroad, the couple's move to San Francisco, and the birth of their son, Daniel. Daniel's parents die in the earthquake of 1906. The story continues to the 1930's, focusing on Daniel's rise to success as a shipping magnate and his marriage to a prominent banker's daughter, Jean Seldon. As the years pass, the story also portrays the lives of other immigrant groups—Chinese, Jewish, Irish—and the growth of cities on the West Coast. During the Depression, Daniel loses his fortune—but gains love through a second marriage and reconciliation with his estranged daughter.

HOWARD FAST (1914–   )
The Second Generation (1978; 438 PAGES; D/M)

This is the second in a series dealing with the immigrant Lavette family. The story opens in 1934, as Dan Lavette leaves his fishing boat and goes home to San Francisco where his second wife, the Chinese May Ling, awaits him. This volume focuses on Barbara Lavette, the daughter of Dan and his first wife, socialite Jean Seldon. Barbara, troubled by her mother's social world and caught between her parents' two heritages, begins to build a life of her own in pre-World-War-II Europe. In this setting, she sees the growth of Nazism, the course of the war, her father's role in Democratic politics, and (when she returns to the United States) the postwar period of business boom.

HOWARD FAST (1914–   )
The Outsiders (1984; 311 PAGES; M/D)

This story unfolds from 1946 to the 1960's, a period of sweeping social changes. Rabbi David Hartmann arrives in Leighton, Connecticut, in 1946 to serve fourteen Jewish families and to help build a synagogue. Having survived World War II, Rabbi Hartmann looks forward to small-town life, which he believes will be wholesome, uncomplicated, and peaceful. Instead, he finds the town full of bigotry, prejudice, and intolerance. The attitudes of the townspeople slowly change as anti-Communist McCarthyism, the civil rights and women's movements, and the Vietnam War explode across America. Not least affected by the changing social climate are the rabbi and his wife and family. As is often the case, change seems frightening but can also lead to a new way of life. This happens to the townspeople and to the rabbi, who leaves his wife for another woman.

EDNA FERBER (1887–1968)
Cimarron (1929; 388 PAGES; M/M)

Cimarron begins with one of the great episodes in the history of the American West: the opening of Oklahoma to land settlement, made possible by one of the U.S. government's land acts in 1889. The Venable family, transplanted southerners, decide to go to Oklahoma (a Choctaw Indian word meaning "red people"). Sabra Venable marries Yancey Cravat, an adventurer intent on claiming some choice land. Their lives, that of their son Cim, and those of all of the assorted Indians, gamblers, settlers, Mexicans, and oil men are dramatically woven into a narrative of Oklahoma's journey to statehood.

EDNA FERBER (1887–1968)
Giant (1952; 447 PAGES; D/D)

Leslie Lynnton has been raised in a gracious, intellectual environment in Virginia in the 1920's. When handsome Texan Jordan Benedict visits on business, she decides to marry him and move to Texas. Nothing prepares Leslie for the harsh living conditions of this vast land. Leslie is shocked by her husband's and others' treatment of Mexican workers—who work slavishly for others on land that once belonged to their ancestors. After the oil boom and its resulting wealth, ranching takes a backseat in Texas. Mexican citizens demand better pay and living conditions, while Benedict and his friends plot to keep Mexicans downtrodden. Not until Benedict's only son marries a Mexican and fathers a potential heir does Benedict begin to see Mexicans as people with the same needs as others.

EDNA FERBER (1887–1968)
Great Son (1945; 271 PAGES; M/M)

A rich tale spanning nearly a century (1851–1941), *Great Son* chronicles the lives of the Melendy family, Seattle's oldest and most prosperous family. The novel covers widely varying topics including the settlement of Seattle, the importing of women from the eastern U.S. to serve as wives for settlers, the Alaskan gold frontier, a refugee fleeing Nazi Germany, the onset of World War II, and the subtle yet volatile Melendy family secrets, emotions, prejudices, and moral character. Romance, politics, history, and social dynamics are present throughout *Great Son*.

EDNA FERBER (1887–1968)
Show Boat (1926; ABOUT 302 PAGES; M/M)

Known mostly for the love story between Magnolia Hawks and Gaylord Ravenal, *Show Boat* also presents an interpretation of riverboat life on the Mississippi from the 1870's to the 1920's. Magnolia spends her childhood on the showboat *Cotton Blossom,* which plies the river twice a year, stopping at numerous towns along the way to provide entertainment. Magnolia marries Gaylord, a gambler, and their life is spent in Chicago's "Gambler's Alley." Their child, Kim, grows up to become a famous New York City actress on the emerging Broadway stage. A secondary theme—intermarriage between a white man and a woman with African-American ancestry—created strong reaction when the novel was published.

EDNA FERBER (1887–1968)
So Big (1924; 360 PAGES; M/M)

So Big portrays the harsh life and eventual prosperity of a determined woman. In the late 1800's, Miss Selina Peake is the daughter of a moderately successful gambler. She leads a life of relative privilege until her father dies as she is reaching adulthood. Selina decides to teach in a Dutch community a few miles outside Chicago; life there is much harder than she has imagined. Highly independent, Selina challenges the traditional role of women, even after her marriage to a traditional local farmer. Living in poverty the whole of her married life, she defies the standards set for women and creates a prosperous life for her son after her husband's death. She also tries to instill in her son her love of art, culture, and beauty.

ELSIE KIMMELL FIELD
Prairie Winter (1960; 153 PAGES; E/E)

There was a time when Americans could win tracts of land through a government lottery. Near the turn of the twentieth century, train engineer Benjamin Kimmell and his family live in Iowa. Mr. Kimmell dreams of moving west and having a farm. His dreams come true when he draws a winning number for land near McIntosh, South Dakota, on the Standing Rock Reservation. He and the family—with the dogs, the cow, and the piano—pack up and go west on the train. Once in South Dakota, the Kimmells become homesteaders. If they build a house and farm successfully, their claim will turn into ownership in one year. During the year, the family experiences all of the joys and hard work of homesteading.

RACHEL FIELD (1894–1942)
Calico Bush (1931; ABOUT 199 PAGES; M/M)

In 1743, a ship brings the Sargent family from Massachusetts to the coast of Maine to begin a new life on a claim. Along with them comes Marguerite, now called Maggie, who is French. She has lost all of her family in transit to the New World, so she has become an indentured servant—a "bound-out" girl—to the family. When the family arrives at their new home, they experience many hardships of daily pioneer living, including the threat of Indian attack. As the seasons pass, Maggie becomes increasingly resourceful and valuable to the family during many crises. Finally, she has to make the important decision about whether to stay or return to France.

ANN FINLAYSON (1925–   )
Greenhorn on the Frontier (1974; 207 PAGES; M/M)

In the pre-Revolutionary period, colonial Virginia and Pennsylvania had an unsettled boundary. Young Harry Warrilow and his sister Sukey move across the Alleghenies in a quest to find land and build a home on the frontier. They spend some time at Pittsburgh; then they move on to western Pennsylvania, where they choose to stay. Harry and Sukey experience common frontier hardships: severe weather, isolation, lack of law, difficult work, and illness. To add to their problems, the Warrilows are caught in the complex relations between colonial Virginia and Pennsylvania, both claiming some of the same land. The swirl of Revolutionary events also involves the Warrilows.

ANN FINLAYSON (1925–   )
Rebecca's War (1972; 269 PAGES; M/M)

By 1777, the Revolutionary War had taken a bad turn for the American side. This novel examines the occupation of Philadelphia by the British, seen through the eyes of fourteen-year-old Rebecca Ransome. For the eight and a half months of the occupation, Rebecca is the head of the household (all of the adults are away fighting). She is faced with providing food for her brother and sister. The house is also occupied—first by one British officer, then by a second officer who is severely wounded. Rebecca meets the challenges of feeding the family, dealing with the officers, and—most important—delivering an urgent message and gold to American troops.

LEONARD EVERETT FISHER (1924–   )
The Warlock of Westfall (1974; 116 PAGES; E/E)

Not all of the witches persecuted in Salem were women. This novel tells the story of Samuel Swift, a bachelor in his seventies who lives in Westfall, Massachusetts, in 1692. This is the period of the near-mass witchcraft hysteria that swept through New England. Since he is a recluse and lonely, Samuel invents a family and constructs small grave markers for them near his isolated house. The discovery of these markers by a group of boys leads to a startling series of events. Samuel is tried as a warlock (a male witch), convicted, and executed. Then into the scene comes Samuel's brother, Nathan, who is not supposed to exist.

F. SCOTT FITZGERALD (1896–1940)
The Great Gatsby (1925; ABOUT 186 PAGES; M/M)

Mysterious Jay Gatsby has been an enduring American literary character since Fitzgerald created him, Daisy Buchanan, and a host of other 1920's personalities with the publication of this novel. *The Great Gatsby* is of historical interest because of Fitzgerald's portrayals of the lives and times of the "Jazz Age." These portrayals have endured until the present as a representation of the empty, purposeless, and rather decadent lives of the rich in an era of little taxation. Significant for its style and reflection of the atmosphere of the period, *The Great Gatsby* depicts eastern Long Island society in an era of excess.

JOHN D. FITZGERALD (1907?–1988)
Brave Buffalo Fighter (1973; 179 PAGES; E/E)

Based on the diary of Susan Parker, *Brave Buffalo Fighter* tells of a family's experiences as they travel to the American West. In 1860, when Susan is ten, her parents and her brother, Jerry, leave St. Joseph, Missouri, for a life farther west. On the way to Fort Laramie, Wyoming, the wagon train suffers problems of illness, death, fights, and frustration. Unusual incidents of bravery and sacrifice occur as the story progresses. At one point, Native Americans observe Jerry as he kills a bull buffalo. After the Native Americans attack the wagon train, they offer peace if Jerry will come with them to be a son to their chief. Jerry does this—against his parents' wishes—and not until sixteen years later do they learn his fate.

PAUL FLEISCHMAN (1952–   )
Bull Run (1993; 102 PAGES; E/M)

The first battle of the Civil War, fought in 1861 at Bull Run, Manassas, Virginia, is the setting of this novel. The war affects many people in different ways. A black man pretends to be white in order to become a soldier in the Union Army. A photographer enjoys a booming business traveling with soldiers and charging them to immortalize their likenesses for loved ones back home. A buggy driver is hired to carry well-dressed and happy passengers to witness the battle at Bull Run; they have packed picnic baskets and brought champagne. A doctor is amazed by how shocked soldiers are when their targets bleed and die—as if death is not what the mock battles and practice drills have been about. A slave girl serving her master on the battlefield plots escape to the North. These and other perspectives on the war comprise this unusual narrative.

INGLIS FLETCHER (1879–1969)
The Wind in the Forest (1956; 443 PAGES; D/D)

The Wind in the Forest features two prominent individuals in the history of North Carolina. In 1768 North Carolina is divided between the conservative planters of the eastern tidewater area and the frontier farmers of the western counties. The leader of the planters is the Royal Governor, William Tryon. The leader of the farmers is a quiet Quaker, Harmon Husband. The farmers feel that the governor supports unequal laws and discriminatory taxes, which make it difficult to keep the land. Tryon feels that Husband's pamphlets and the farmers' petitions are acts of defiance. The two sides meet in the Battle of Alamance in 1771, in which the farmers are defeated.

JANE FLORY (1917–   )
The Liberation of Clementine Tipton (1974; 213 PAGES; E/E)

Ten-year-old Clementine Tipton and her family live in a mansion in Philadelphia, where the great International Centennial Exposition is to be held. The Exposition will celebrate the one hundredth birthday of the United States in 1876. Clementine is more concerned with the selection of her new governess, for her last one was mean and insulting. Miss Lamb, though, is kind and very intelligent. More importantly for Clementine, she is also a feminist. Miss Lamb is from England and is anxious to be in America for the Exposition, at which the Women's Pavilion will be a prominent feature. For the first time in her life, Clementine is treated with the same respect and regard for her future as are the boys. Although her mother is content to be a society matron and her father opposes women's rights, Clementine asserts her intention to enter the new century as an educated and useful woman. This story encompasses women's rights and the lives of upper-class Americans and their servants in the nineteenth century.

ESTHER FORBES (1891–1967)
Johnny Tremain (1943; 256 PAGES; M/M)

One of the most honored of historical novels, *Johnny Tremain* chronicles two years (1773–1775) in the life of a young silversmith's apprentice in Boston. Johnny is fourteen, bright, and somewhat arrogant. Well on the way to becoming a silversmith and eventually marrying a daughter of his "adopted" family, Johnny suffers a horrible accident when molten silver spills over his hand and maims it. Now he must search for work. Eventually, he becomes a delivery rider for the Committee of Correspondence in Boston. He comes into contact with the famous Boston patriots and participates in the Tea Party and Battle of Lexington. On the battlefield, a doctor tells Johnny that his injured hand can be repaired and that he will be able to hold a musket and fight.

JESSE HILL FORD (1928–)
The Raider (1975; 463 PAGES; D/M)

In the spare language of a sparsely written style, Tennessee native Ford writes about a large cast of characters. Elias McCutcheon is at the center—before, during, and after the Civil War in west Tennessee. Elias comes into the area alone to stake a claim in the 1830's, a time when the Chickasaw Indians still manage the land. With their help and his own talents, McCutcheon forges a frontier community, only to see it burned during the war and the northern troop occupation. With determination, he returns and rebuilds. Surrounding McCutcheon are his sons and wife, a wealthy Chickasaw chief, an outlaw, a speculator, and various neighbors.

JAMES FORMAN (1932–)
The Life and Death of Yellow Bird (1973; 212 PAGES; M/M)

When General George Custer fought Indians at the Battle of Washita, he took captive an Indian princess. She bore Custer a son, who was raised by his mother and named Yellow Bird. This account imagines the life of Yellow Bird from the time shortly before the Battle of the Little Bighorn, Montana (where Custer was killed in 1876) until Yellow Bird's death in 1890 at the Battle of Wounded Knee, South Dakota. In the story Chief Crazy Horse takes Yellow Bird under his own wing and, with him, endures being hunted by the white men. Yellow Bird also travels to New York and to London as part of western star Bill Cody's Wild West Show. The author's careful choice of language suggests that the book might have been written by an English-speaking Indian.

ED FOSTER
Tejanos (1970; 48 PAGES; E/E)

Tejanos is the story of two brother who were actually involved in the battle of the Alamo in Houston, Texas, in 1836. The brothers, Gregorio and Francisco Esparza, and Gregorio's son Enrique, are descendants of a Spanish military family. They are *Tejanos*, or Mexican citizens of Texas. Gregorio and Francisco are fighting against each other in the battle over how Texas should be governed. Gregorio, Enrique's father, disdains the bloody tactics of Santa Anna, general of the Mexican Centralist army invading Texas. Gregorio wants an independent, self-ruling Texas, not one ruled by the dictatorial Santa Anna. Francisco sides with Santa Anna. Eleven-year-old Enrique watches as his father is killed when Santa Anna and his army, including Francisco, overtake the Alamo. The introduction to this story includes a concise explanation of the politics involved in the battle between Texas and Mexico.

JAMES R. FRENCH
Nauvoo (1982; 302 PAGES; M/M)

Nauvoo is the name of a city in Illinois on the banks of the Mississippi. It was founded in the 1840's by members of the Church of Jesus Christ of Latter Day Saints—the Mormons. This novel follows the plight of the Mormons who sought to escape persecution and set up their church without interference. Using actual background events and facts about the founders of the Church, Joseph Smith and Brigham Young, the author creates imaginary characters to explore the arrival of the Mormons in Nauvoo. Included in the story are the building of the city, the bitter fighting between Mormons and non-Mormons, the revocation of the city charter by the state, the decline of the city, and the decision to move to the Great Salt Lake in Utah. The author provides an important account of a little-studied chapter in American history.

JEAN FRITZ (1915–   )
Brady (1960; 223 PAGES; M/M)

In Pennsylvania in 1836, Brady Minton, the son of an abolitionist preacher, is a good, honest boy, but he has trouble keeping secrets. The only secret he can keep is that he hates killing or hurting animals—a trait he fears makes him appear unmanly. When Brady and his best friend go hunting, they stumble upon a cabin being used as an Underground Railroad station. Brady eagerly tells his father, who is surprisingly distant and remote. His brother, Matt, explains that Brady is treating lightly a life-and-death matter. Runaway slaves could be returned, and even killed, if caught. Determined to earn his father's trust and respect, Brady decides to deliver a runaway slave to the next underground station.

JEAN FRITZ (1915–   )
The Cabin Faced West (1958; 115 PAGES; E/E)

When Ann Hamilton and her pioneer family move west in the 1880's, the "West" is not very far away. In the early years of westward movement, the Allegheny Mountains were a great barrier to pioneers. After leaving Gettysburg, the family journeys beyond the Alleghenies into western Pennsylvania. Here, at Hamilton Hill in the 1780's, the family works hard to settle and make a living out of the land. Young Ann misses her old life and relatives and is quite unhappy. Then a series of people come into her life and make her realize how worthwhile her new life can be. Not least among the visitors, in 1784, is George Washington.

JEAN FRITZ (1915–)
Early Thunder (1967; 242 PAGES; M/M)

This story takes place in 1775, in Salem, Massachusetts, the capital of the colony and thus a strategic place in trying times. Daniel West, the son of the local doctor, is a Tory—a person who is loyal to the king and England. Others in Salem are Whigs or Patriots—those who want to break loose from England. Daniel's story traces a path of changing loyalties; he gradually comes to believe in the Whig cause. At the same time, he struggles to adjust to the death of his mother and to the new wife his father brings home from Boston. Daniel's personal and political struggles merge when the British come to Salem one day and Daniel chooses to defy them.

DORIS GATES (1901–1987)
Blue Willow (1940; ABOUT 159 PAGES; E/E)

A long-time favorite, *Blue Willow* is the story of a family of migrant workers in the San Joaquin Valley in California in the 1930's. Down on his luck, Mr. Larkin has moved his family many times in the past five years since they left Texas. Now living with his family in an abandoned house on a large landowner's property, Larkin works in the cotton fields and in the irrigation ditches. Ten-year-old Janey Larkin meets another migrant family, the Romeros, and she and Lupe Romero become good friends. The Larkins seek a stable life. They live by basic values—symbolized by a blue willow plate, a remnant of a past life, which provides the underlying theme in the novel.

PATRICIA LEE GAUCH (1934–)
Thunder at Gettysburg (1975; 46 PAGES; E/E)

Young Tillie Pierce, like others in and around Gettysburg on July 1, 1863, decides to watch the excitement when a Rebel infantry encounters a Union cavalry and a fierce battle breaks out. She watches from her attic window and looks forward to an entertaining time. Instead, though, Tillie is caught up in the awful action of Americans killing Americans. She is quickly drafted into service caring for wounded Union soldiers. When the battle is finally over and the Rebels sag away in defeat, Tillie finds no joy in the Union victory. She just wants to be reunited with her family and have peace and quiet. No one in Gettysburg again thinks of the war as the sort of afternoon picnic they had so eagerly anticipated only a few days earlier.

LYNNE GESSNER (1919–   )
Navajo Slave (1976; 199 PAGES; M/M)

The focus of this novel is an Indian warrior's adjustment to life in the 1840's as a slave on a Mexican hacienda in U.S. territory. Straight Arrow is the son of Red Band, a Navajo warrior. They live in the Southwest, in New Mexico Territory, at the time of Kit Carson—who makes a business of hunting Indians. In a raid, Red Band dies; Straight Arrow is captured by a Ute Indian, who sells him to Mexicans as a slave. Straight Arrow is now called Nino. As time passes, he develops relationships with Jake, the white overseer, and with Tomos and Miguel, sons of Don Armando, the landowner. Eventually, Nino plots to escape and return home.

JANICE HOLT GILES (1909–1979)
The Kentuckians (1953; ABOUT 248 PAGES; M/M)

People who went to Kentucky in the eighteenth century were among the first real pioneers of the West. At the time, the frontier was the area west of the Allegheny Mountains barrier. Using three fictional characters, the author translates this pioneer experience into a story of settlement and war. David Cooper has traveled the area with Daniel Boone; now he returns to the frontier to settle down and clear land. During the Revolution, the Kentuckians fight against the British and their Native-American allies. The settlers also experience conflict among themselves over legal claims to the land between the Commonwealth of Virginia and the Transylvania Company. The author bases her narrative on journals of the period.

CONNIE JORDAN GREEN (1897–1975)
The War at Home (1989; 136 PAGES; E/E)

The War at Home chronicles daily life in the Oak Ridge mountains, including local reactions to World War II and its destructive end. Thirteen-year-old Mattie McDowell moves with her family from Kentucky to Tennessee to a government-protected community. Her father's work is secret, and Mattie knows only that it concerns the war effort. When her twelve-year-old cousin Virgil comes to live with them, he irritates Mattie with his male chauvinism. But, as the war comes to a close, Mattie's perception of her problems changes. With the knowledge that her father's work involves building the atomic bomb—responsible for the killing of thousands of Japanese, but also speeding the end of the war—Mattie puts her problems into perspective.

BETTE GREENE (1934–)
Summer of My German Soldier (1973; 230 PAGES; M/M)

In a small town in Arkansas in 1941, Patty Bergen is far removed from war-torn Germany and its dictator, Adolf Hitler, whose hate campaign is in full force. Twelve-year-old Patty is intelligent, sensitive, Jewish, and utterly unloved by her parents. Her black nanny, Ruth, seems more like a real mother and is her only friend. Patty shelters a German prisoner of war who has escaped from a nearby camp. Anton is not a Nazi; he speaks fluent English and is kind to Patty. When Anton leaves, Patty is devastated. Shortly thereafter, she is arrested and sent to reform school for harboring the enemy. Suddenly, a reverse version of the hate campaign waged against Jews by Hitler is waged against her. Patty learns that intolerance, bigotry, fear, and ignorance can propel the quiet southern town. From Ruth, she also learns about dignity, self-respect, and love devoid of social, economic, racial, or religious barriers.

KRISTIANA GREGORY (1951–)
Earthquake at Dawn (1992; 185 PAGES; M/M)

In 1906, San Francisco, California, was hit by a tremendous earthquake. Twenty-two-year-old Edith Irvine, a photographer, is caught in the city en route to a photography exhibition in Europe when the quake occurs. Stranded in San Francisco with her companion, Daisy, Edith is an eyewitness to the damage caused by the quake and subsequent fires. The mayor and his political cronies are desperate to cover up and underestimate the death toll and property damage; they forbid photographers and journalists to tell the real story. Edith takes photographs secretly and hides them away for years. They are not revealed until research uncovers the true story, and the actual death toll, property damage, and political corruption are made public.

KRISTIANA GREGORY (1951–)
Jenny of the Tetons (1989; 114 PAGES; E/M)

Each chapter of this book is prefaced with an entry from the actual journals of Beaver Dick Leigh, an English trapper and guide in the Teton Mountain area of Idaho in the late nineteenth century. Leigh was married to a remarkable Shoshone Indian named Jenny. (Until 1929 and the conversion of the Tetons into a state park, two lakes situated there bore the names Beaver Dick Lake and Jenny Lake.) In the book, fifteen-year-old Carrie Hill is orphaned when her parents are murdered in 1875 by hostile American Indians. Carrie agrees to live with Beaver Dick and his family—only to be filled with alarm and hatred when she discovers that Dick's wife, Jenny, is an Indian. Jenny explains that her own beloved mother was murdered by hostile whites, but that just as all whites are not bad, neither are all Indians. The real Jenny Leigh died in 1876, at the age of twenty-seven, as a result of caring for friends afflicted with a deadly pox.

ARNOLD A. GRIESE (1921–)
The Way of Our People (1975; 82 PAGES; E/E)

This story takes place in 1838 in the Native-American village of Anvik, near the western coast of Alaska, when it was still owned by Russia. As the story opens, thirteen-year-old Kano has just killed his first moose—a major test of becoming an adult in the eyes of his village. However, Kano has a great fear of being in the forest; he must spend many months alone conquering his fear and learning how to hunt. In the meantime, smallpox comes to the area. Kano meets a Russian named Ivan, who has medicine to prevent this white man's disease. Native Americans still live in the village of Anvik today.

WINSTON GROOM (1943–)
Better Times Than These (1978; 411 PAGES; D/D)

The author (a Vietnam veteran) creates a compelling portrait of a group of men in Bravo Company, Fourth Battalion, Seventh Cavalry. They ship out to Vietnam, organize on the ground, and participate in patrols and holding actions against the enemy. Along with these events, the author describes stateside activities. During the course of the novel, most of the themes of the Vietnam War are introduced: reasons for the war, questioning the war, antiwar activities, conditions of fighting on the ground, interaction among the men, and relationships with the Vietnamese. This is a "worm's-eye" view of the war by men who fought it and then wondered why. The climax of the action is a disastrous encounter by the company. The novel contains graphic language and situations perhaps not suitable for some readers.

MARY DOWNING HAHN (1937–)
December Stillness (1990; 181 PAGES; E/M)

This novel focuses on the continued emotional problems suffered by many Vietnam War veterans. Kelly's high-school teacher assigns the students a paper on current social issues. Deciding on homelessness, Kelly focuses on Bob Weems, a homeless Vietnam vet who spends his days at the public library. Although her father—also a Vietnam vet—tries to dissuade her, Kelly persists in trying to help Mr. Weems. Weems meets her approaches with hostility, and because of her, he is soon barred from the library. He is later killed in a car accident. Kelly is left to find some way to conquer her guilt and to understand better the psychology of the homeless and of veterans of the Vietnam War.

ALEX HALEY (1921–1992)
A Different Kind of Christmas (1988; 101 PAGES; M/M)

Until the winter of 1855, Fletcher Randall has spent every Christmas of his life as heir-apparent to his wealthy father, a North Carolina state senator and plantation owner. This, though, will be a different kind of Christmas for Fletcher. Previously a staunch defender of slavery, Fletcher has changed his mind while attending the College of New Jersey. There he has met three Quaker brothers, who introduce him to their views on slavery—an institution they strongly oppose. The brothers take Fletcher home with them to Philadelphia, where for the first time he encounters free African Americans. Still unconvinced that black people are really human, Fletcher is enlightened when he reads a speech by former slave Frederick Douglass. Back home in North Carolina for Christmas, Fletcher secretly works for the Underground Railroad. Stealing away to the North with an escaped slave (thereby breaching the Fugitive Slave Act), Fletcher must face the fact that his family will now consider him a traitor.

WALTER (1901–1984) AND MARION HAVIGHURST (1894–1974)
Song of the Pines (1949; ABOUT 205 PAGES; E/E)

The hard work, disappointments, and hopes of a new ethnic group in America make up this engaging story. Fifteen-year-old Nils Thorson leaves Norway in the mid-nineteenth century to make his way to the Wisconsin Territory. The story chronicles the voyage to America, the trip overland, Nils's acquaintance with the Svendsen family, and his early attempts to find a job as a knife grinder. Nils finds work in the store of Mr. Martin, who becomes a trusted friend. Nils then sets out to lumbering country, where he learns a new trade as he becomes acquainted with the lumber industry.

NATHANIEL HAWTHORNE (1804–1864)
The House of the Seven Gables (1851; ABOUT 261 PAGES; M/D)

Not a historical novel on the surface, Hawthorne's work nonetheless can be read for historical insights. Part of the novel is set near the time when Hawthorne lived, in the mid-nineteenth century, and part is set in the seventeenth century. In the story a seventeenth-century curse works itself out on four characters: Hepzibah, Phoebe, Clifford, and Joffrey. The novel provides much depth and a variety of details about nineteenth-century American life in a New England town, including social comments on class structure in America.

NATHANIEL HAWTHORNE (1804–1864)
The Scarlet Letter (1850; ABOUT 237 PAGES; M/M)

Three intertwined lives—those of Hester Prynne, Roger Chillingworth, and Reverend Arthur Dimmesdale—form a moral and historical tale that is one of the most famous in American fiction. Set in the period 1642–1649 in Salem, Massachusetts, *The Scarlet Letter* recounts the story of Hester—who commits adultery, bears a child named Pearl, and is forced to wear the letter *A* all the rest of her days. As a classic of American fiction, this can be read on a purely literary level, as a symbolic work, and as a moral treatise. Historically, it provides a wonderful picture of New England Puritan life in the mid-seventeenth century, complete with many historical references by Hawthorne.

J. M. HAYES (1919–)
The Grey Pilgrim (1990; 218 PAGES; D/D)

The last American Indian uprising occurred in October 1940 in Arizona. The cause of the uprising was the intention of the United States government to draft American Indians into the army. *The Grey Pilgrim* is based on the events surrounding this uprising. The Papagos Indians and their aged leader, Jujul, refuse to fight for a country that refuses them citizenship. When an inept bureaucrat from Indian Affairs causes an unnecessary gunfight, Deputy U.S. Marshall J.D. Fitzpatrick is sent to look for and arrest the fleeing Indians. Unsure where to look, Fitzpatrick enlists the aid of a young female student specializing in Papago history and customs. Jujul is finally arrested and jailed after a gruesome and complicated chase. The catalyst for this chase is the unlikely presence of a murderous Japanese army officer, whose mission is to stir the Native Americans to continued revolt—thereby diverting attention from the Japanese threat in the Pacific. (The presence of the Japanese officer is not historical.) Violence, adult language, and adult situations are prevalent.

BETSY HAYNES (1937–)
Cowslip (1973; 132 PAGES; E/E)

This novel begins in 1861, just prior to the War Between the States. Cowslip is the name of a thirteen-year-old black girl who has come from Missouri to Kentucky and is now to be sold on the auction block. She enters into a swirling atmosphere of talk of war, rumblings about freedom for African Americans, discovery of what the Underground Railroad means, and the escape of slaves. Although Cowslip becomes a house slave (a higher status than field hand) and has a kind mistress, she is still treated harshly by the master. By the end of the novel, she comes to learn what freedom means and what it is to be an individual, despite the fact that she is still a slave.

WILMA PITCHFORD HAYS (1909–)
The Scarlet Badge (1963; 106 PAGES; E/E)

Most American Revolutionary War tales focus on the colonists and their struggle for independence. Few explore the feelings and struggles of the Loyalists—those who remained loyal to England and the king and thought that the conflicts could be worked out peacefully. The Loyalist story is explored in this novel through the character of Rob Roberts, a young Virginian whose family has been on this land for 150 years. As events unfold in 1775 and 1776, Rob's father must go to England. Rob must come to grips with his loyalty—considered treason by the revolutionaries—and with longtime friends who have become enemies. Rob, too, leaves for England, but he is determined to return to Virginia.

MARCY HEIDISH (1947–)
Miracles (1984; 303 PAGES; D/D)

Elizabeth Bayley Seton was canonized in 1975 as the first American-born saint. Born in the late eighteenth century, Seton grew up as an Episcopalian in a wealthy New York City family. She married happily, and bore five children. After the death of her husband, however, she underwent a spiritual change and converted to Catholicism—in an age of prejudice against Catholics. Eventually, Seton became a nun. She moved into wilderness areas with a group of women who became the first order of American Catholic sisters, located in Maryland. Credited with founding the American parochial school system, Seton is investigated in this novel by a fictional modern priest who follows her life. He examines Seton's involvement in the incidents of miracles which the Catholic Church requires as qualifications for sainthood.

JOSEPH HELLER (1923–)
Catch-22 (1961; 456 PAGES; M/M)

A major literary sensation when it first appeared, *Catch-22* continues to be an important statement about the ridiculous nature of war. A handful of World War II pilots are based on the island of Pianosa in the Mediterranean Sea near Italy. Centered on the character of Captain Yossarian, the novel proceeds along three basic fronts. First, the activities of Yossarian at the base are chronicled. He moves in and out of the base hospital trying to avoid flying missions, but he is confronted with "clean" wounded men. The second theme is the account of the bombing missions, during which many men are killed not so cleanly. Finally, Yossarian's private-life exploits—which concentrate on interacting with women—are detailed. A stream of characters who meet with Yossarian parade through the novel until he, caught in the web of the *Catch-22* title, finally goes home. Frank language, sexism, and sexual situations abound; thus this novel should be used carefully in classroom reading.

JOHN HERSEY (1914–1993)
A Bell for Adano (1944; ABOUT 266 PAGES; M/M)

This was Hersey's first novel, written after he gained fame as a war correspondent. The idea for the story came from Hersey's experiences in the Mediterranean in 1943. He wanted the book to be a lesson about how American soldiers—many still first-generation Americans—could and should act once the troops reached Europe. The story focuses on Italian-American Major Victor Joppolo, who heads the American occupation unit in an Italian town called Adano. The town's ancient bell was taken by the Nazis. Now the townspeople's greatest wish is for Adano to have a bell again. One of Joppolo's main tasks is to restore the bell, as he also goes about trying to nurture democratic feelings.

JOHN HERSEY (1914–1993)
The Child Buyer (1960; 229 PAGES; M/D)

Through the format of testimonial hearings, Hersey introduces and explores all of the characters in this drama—and at the same time explores the values in a society. In the town of Pequot, in an unknown state in the 1950's, a state senate standing committee on education, welfare, and public morality meets to consider the case of Mr. Wissey Jones. An unassuming type who eventually reveals chilling intentions, Mr. Jones is in Pequot to buy the boy Barry Rudd for an experiment. This experiment will improve the nation through buying gifted children and reducing them, through drugs and surgery, to thinking machines without pasts, families, or emotions.

JAMES HICKEY (1907–)
Chrysanthemum in the Snow (1990; 333 PAGES; D/D)

In 1950, South Korea was invaded by North Korea. Because South Korea was an American client nation, America became involved. The story of Lieutenant Donald Robertson unfolds against this background. In 1952, he is leader of an infantry rifle platoon in the Korean War. The requisite soldiers' conversation of sexual conquest and denigration of women now leaves the once-participatory Robertson cold. For Robertson the war has become a personal hell, as he relives his rape and murder of a young Korean virgin. Neither his deep love for a few fellow officers nor the affections of an Army nurse console him. Eventually awarded promotions, medals, and hero status, Robertson keeps his offense a secret from the officials. To punish himself, he returns unnecessarily to the front and is killed. The novel discusses the military and political interrelationships among the United States, North and South Korea, and China, with a focus on the uselessness of the war. Sexual situations and language are present.

JANET HICKMAN (1940–)
The Valley of the Shadow (1974; 212 PAGES; M/M)

Tobias is a thirteen-year-old Delaware Native American boy. He is one of the group of Christian Delawares converted by Moravian missionaries, who founded settlements in southeast Ohio in the period before the Revolution. Moravian Church members are pacifists (opposed to war), and as the Revolutionary War rages on, the Moravians and their Delaware friends make every effort to remain neutral and treat the wounded on both sides. However, the geographical position of the settlements puts Tobias and his tribespeople, as well as the missionaries, at great risk between the colonists and the British. In one of the great tragedies of the war, colonists kill several dozen Delawares at Gnadenhutten, but Tobias escapes.

JANET HICKMAN (1940–)
Zoar Blue (1978; 137 PAGES; E/E)

Today, the Zoar community in Ohio exists only as a group of empty buildings and a few businesses kept intact by the historical society and tourists. In 1861, when this story begins, Zoar was a bustling community. Founded by German Separatists in 1817, Zoar prospered for most of the nineteenth century and was disbanded in 1898. At the time of the novel, the Civil War is beginning and has a great impact on the isolated, pacifist community. The focus is on thirteen-year-old Barbara Hoff and seventeen-year-old John Keffer. Barbara runs away to Pennsylvania to find a lost relative and John enlists in the Union Army. Aspects of Civil War history, life in Zoar, and the theme of adolescents' search for identity are woven together.

JAMAKE HIGHWATER (1942?–)
Eyes of Darkness (1983; 189 PAGES; M/M)

In the 1870's, a boy named Yesa is raised by his elderly grandmother, Uncheedah. She teaches him the ways of the People of the Plains, the American Indians of Minnesota. Yesa hears that his father has been killed; he yearns to be a great warrior to avenge his death. Ten years later, Yesa's father suddenly reappears, wearing the clothes of the white man and preaching the words of the white man's Jesus. Yesa must adopt his father's new Christian name of East, and so becomes Alexander East. He must also go with his father to a mission and learn to live as a white. He decides that he can save people by teaching them to live in white society and to assimilate rather than resist. Alexander attends Dartmouth College and becomes a medical doctor after graduating from Boston University. While working on an Indian reservation, Alexander is called upon to attend to soldiers injured in the Battle of Wounded Knee. After years of being a victim of bigotry and then witnessing the brutality toward Indians at Wounded Knee, Alexander realizes that whites will never allow Native Americans to live peaceably among them.

LAURA Z. HOBSON (1900–1986)
Gentleman's Agreement (1947; ABOUT 275 PAGES; M/M)

Gentleman's Agreement chronicles anti-Semitism in the United States. Journalist Phil Green is a widower who has just arrived in New York. He is fresh from California and military duty at the end of World War II. His editor gives him a knotty assignment: He is to write a weekly series about anti-Semitism, or prejudice against Jewish people. Green wrestles for weeks for an angle, and then decides to pretend he is Jewish. As the weeks go by, he encounters the subtle as well as the direct discrimination that Jews encounter: barred entrances to clubs, hotels, and restaurants; social snubs, inflammatory language. His fiancée, his mother, and his young son also become involved in the arrangement. His series succeeds and becomes a book. However, his and his family's lives are changed forever.

CECILIA HOLLAND (1943–)
The Bear Flag (1990; 419 PAGES; D/D)

The Bear Flag was raised in Sonoma, California, on June 14, 1846. California at the time was a vast territory inhabited by Native Americans, adventurers, settlers, and *Californios,* the Mexicans who governed the land. The novel explores the cultures of these diverse groups. Cat Reilly is a transplanted widow from Boston. He is an integral part of a group who want to form California into an independent republic rather than the property of either the United Sates or Mexico. This unique democratic experiment fails as John Charles Frémont, Kit Carson, and an expansionist America take over California. After heated battle, the Californios surrender to Frémont—with the warning that the eventual control of California will be decided by the war between Mexico and the United States. *Bear Flag* debunks the heroic status of both Frémont and Carson; both are portrayed as greedy, somewhat villainous characters.

WILLIAM H. HOOKS (1921–)
Crossing the Line (1978; 121 PAGES; E/E)

Relationships between blacks and whites arouse fear and hatred even in the twentieth century. Eleven-year-old Harrison Hawkins comes of age during this story of growing up in rural North Carolina in the 1930's. Harrison is white; his two friends Serap and Kitty Fisher are a black sister and brother whose family sharecrops on the land. Little Hattie, a mysterious black woman, is also Harrison's friend. She fills the gaps in his education—teaching him especially how blacks and whites in the community are related to each other by more than economic or social class. Deep-seated racial tensions come to the surface as Harrison, Serap, and Kitty set out to solve a mystery surrounding Little Hattie when she disappears.

WILLIAM H. HOOKS (1921–)
Circle of Fire (1982; 144 PAGES; E/E)

This is the continuing story of Harrison Hawkins, an eleven-year-old white boy who lives in the tidewater country of North Carolina in 1936. His best friends, Serap Fisher and her brother Kitty, are black. Around Christmastime, a band of Irish gypsies come into the area, and Harrison becomes interested in the gypsies and their customs. The Ku Klux Klan also becomes interested in the Irish gypsies, for they are Catholic—one of the groups which the Klan hates. As the children learn, the Ku Klux Klan wages hate campaigns against groups other than African Americans. Harrison learns of a planned attack on the gypsies. He, along with Kitty and Serap, worry about how to stop the attack. The tensions and interrelationships among these groups still exist today, since gypsies still come into North Carolina and the Klan still exists.

ELIZABETH HOWARD
Out of Step with the Dancers (1978; 213 PAGES; E/E)

The Shaker, or True Believer, way of life is now preserved in only a few buildings and villages in some parts of the United States. Among other beliefs, Shakers follow a rule of celibacy, or no marriage between men and women in the community. This guarantees that, without continual new converts, the communities will die out. In 1853, in the Shaker village of New Lebanon in New York State, Damaris and her family come as new applicants. It is Damaris's father who has converted and brought his family. Damaris remains opposed to this way of life. As Shaker customs and beliefs are introduced to her, she must make up her mind whether to stay or to leave the community.

ELIZABETH HOWARD
The Courage of Bethea (1959; 248 PAGES; M/M)

A girl's quest for education and a career highlight this novel. Bethea Clinton is a sixteen-year-old girl who lives in Michigan with her father (a minister) and their family. In 1859, her father dies suddenly and the family must separate. Bethea goes to an aunt and uncle who treat her well, but Bethea longs for a reunited family. By chance, she learns that she can attend Western Seminary for Women in Oxford, Ohio, because she is a minister's daughter. With dreams of education and an eventual position teaching, Bethea begins school. The rest of the novel focuses on her schooling, adjustment to the other girls, first meetings with male admirers, and her mother's remarriage.

WILLIAM DEAN HOWELLS (1837–1920)
The Rise of Silas Lapham (1885; ABOUT 321 PAGES; D/D)

Social history dominates this novel. Howells depicts, in realistic fashion, the rise of a newly rich and upwardly mobile class in the post–Civil War era in Boston. The focus of the book is on the character of self-made man Silas Lapham—who, by chance, discovers a key mineral ingredient for paint and becomes a millionaire. Mrs. Lapham meets Mrs. Corey, member of a prominent family, who persuades the Laphams to move into the fashionable section of Boston. This move, the subsequent burning of their new house, financial difficulties, and Lapham's temptation to cheat land-buyers reflect Lapham's struggle to remain a moral person. A second theme—one of manners—involves the romance and marriage of Lapham's daughter and the Coreys' son, a marriage which tries to bridge two classes.

IRENE HUNT (1907–)
Across Five Aprils (1964; 216 PAGES; M/M)

In April 1861, news of the attack on Fort Sumter in the Carolinas comes to the Matthew Creighton family in southern Illinois. From that time on, over the next five Aprils, the family is consumed by the events of the Civil War. Jethro, who is nine years old, assumes greater and greater responsibility as his brothers and cousin leave for the war. One brother joins the Confederate forces; the Creighton family come under suspicion as sympathizers for the South in an area where loyalties can go either way. As the Aprils pass, news of the various battles and his family's part in them comes to Jethro via letters and messengers.

IRENE HUNT (1907–)
Claws of a Young Century (1980; 292 PAGES; M/M)

The turn of the century through World War I (1900–1918) is the time period of this novel. Ellen Archer is seventeen when her story begins on her father's farm in Minnesota. This is an era of great events all over the world, as well as in America. Ellen decides to devote her life to the cause of women's rights. Her brother Alex is determined to improve the practice of medicine. Ellen marries Philip Wrenn, who is a foreign correspondent and abroad much of the time. Ellen and Philip disagree over her role in the family and in society. Despite their separation, they both love their daughter, who will inherit the work of her mother and other women. Philip's sister Robbie works as a social worker in Hull House, a significant social-work institution in Chicago.

IRENE HUNT (1907–)
No Promises in the Wind (1970; 216 PAGES; M/M)

"The year 1932 was not a good one in which to be fifteen years old and in close quarters with a hopeless father." This is Josh Grondowski's judgment of the Depression era and the plight of his unemployed father. Like many others of his age and generation, Josh must strike out on his own to make a living and to grow up very fast in a desolate time. Josh and his brother, Joey, enter the world of the hobo. They leave their home in Chicago and travel to Omaha, Nebraska; Baton Rouge, Louisiana; and then finally return to Chicago. Endless journeys, constant hunger, and the occasional kindness of strangers are the ingredients of their frightening time spent as hobos.

EVAN HUNTER (1926–)
The Chisholms (1976; 208 PAGES; M/M)

Concentrating on one family member per chapter, Hunter develops the personalities of the Chisholms. They leave the stingy land of Appalachian Virginia in 1844 and head for the Cumberland Gap on the border of Tennessee, Kentucky, and Virginia—their entranceway to the West. Through the experiences of Hadley, his wife Minerva, three sons, and two daughters, the westward trek takes shape. The Chisholms encounter plains and forests, rafts and rivers, trading posts and dusty towns, Indian attacks and dangerous white men, and illness and hunger. The strong character of the family makes it possible for them to reach California.

DONALD JACKSON (1919–)
Valley Men (1983; M/M)

Thomas Jefferson doubled the size of the United States in 1803 with the purchase of the Louisiana Territory from the French. With both a practical and naturally curious desire to map the area, Jefferson sent out several now-famous expeditions to explore the new addition. Lewis and Clark went up the Missouri, Zebulon Pike headed into the Rockies, and Thomas Freeman traveled up the Red River. Jefferson planned another expedition up the Arkansas River in 1807, but abandoned it for no clear reason. The author draws on his considerable experience as a historian to write a fictional account of how that exploration might have developed. The novel includes a fictional main character—Dr. Raphael Bailey, a young Philadelphia scientist—and many real-life persons.

ANNABEL (1921–   ) AND EDGAR JOHNSON (1912–1990)
The Last Knife (1971; 185 PAGES; M/M)

An unusual novel in both form and content, *The Last Knife* centers on young Rick, who is searching for his brother Howard. Howard has just been released from prison for draft resistance in the late 1960's. Rick comes across a group of Howard's Native-American friends in the mountains near their southwestern home. Throughout the evening and night, the Native Americans recount several tales of various types of dissent against authority in their world as well as in the white world. Rick learns new perspectives on the use of government power, what patriotism means to different people, and how dissent is handled in a free society.

DOUGLAS C. JONES (1924–   )
A Creek Called Wounded Knee (1978; 231 PAGES; M/M)

By 1890, there was no longer a frontier in the United States. Railroads crisscrossed the land, and the Native-American threat seemed over. However, some American Indians refused to live quietly on reservation lands or at Indian agencies. The Lakota Sioux are one of those tribes; their resistance is the heart of this story. Army troops arrive near Wounded Knee, South Dakota, to contain the fighting. Among the companies is the 7th Cavalry, whose earlier members had fought unsuccessfully at the Little Bighorn, Montana, in 1876. Newspapermen come in great numbers to cover the events. The Sioux are led by ailing Chief Big Foot, who wants a peaceful resolution. However, the Army massacres the Sioux in what becomes the last hostile engagement between U.S. troops and Native Americans.

DOUGLAS C. JONES (1924–   )
Elkhorn Tavern (1980; 308 PAGES; M/M)

This book's central event is the Battle of Pea Ridge, an actual battle fought near the settlement of Elkhorn Tavern. In the hill country of Arkansas in the first year of the Civil War, Martin Hasford's family struggles to survive without him while he is away with Confederate forces. His wife Ora, daughter Calpurnia, and son Roman are often caught between sides as civilian bandits prey on unprotected homes. The events of the story are seen primarily through Roman's eyes. Wild Bill Hickok and Philip Sheridan, who were actually involved in the campaign, come into the story; a wounded Union soldier is brought to the Hasford home to be nursed; and Elkhorn Tavern becomes a Union supply depot. Eventually, the action moves off farther to the east, while the Hasfords continue to survive.

DOUGLAS C. JONES (1924–)
Gone the Dreams and Dancing (1984; 323 PAGES; M/M)

In 1875, the remains of the most warlike of all Native-American tribes, the Comanche, came to Fort Sill, Indian Territory (later Oklahoma), to surrender and take up reservation life. Through the narrator, Liverpool Morgan (a Civil War veteran), the chief figure of Kwahadi, a half-white, emerges. Kwahadi is the leader of the Comanches (and is a fictionalized representation of the actual Comanche chief Quanah). With dignity and care, he resigns himself and his people to integration with whites and to the subservient life of the reservation. Morgan helps Kwahadi search for his white mother. Morgan and other characters are followed through the next decade of life in the Indian Territory—which, in 1907, became the Sooner state of Oklahoma.

DOUGLAS C. JONES (1924–)
The Court-Martial of George Armstrong Custer (1976; 288 PAGES; M/M)

What if General Custer had not died on the battlefield at the Little Bighorn in Montana in 1876? That is the premise of this novel, which places Custer near death on the field and brings him to trial in New York City after he recovers from his wounds. The debate is over whether he is a military genius who made a mistake or a glory seeker who risked his soldiers' lives. In the courtroom, the battle is replayed as several surviving witnesses give their versions of what happened. At the end, Custer himself testifies.

WEYMAN JONES (1928–)
Edge of Two Worlds (1968; 127 PAGES; E/E)

A main character in this novel is Sequoyah, a Cherokee Indian, who developed a Cherokee alphabet and written language. In Texas in 1842, young Calvin Harper is on his way east to law school in Boston when his wagon train is attacked by Comanche Indians. He survives the massacre, but barely survives being alone in the desert. Sequoyah finds Calvin, and they strike up an uneasy alliance. Both need each other. The old Indian is searching for the origins of his people, who have by this period been forced to relocate from Tennessee to Oklahoma. Calvin discovers that he must stay to help Sequoyah before he rejoins mainstream society.

JAN JORDAN (1942–)
Give Me the Wind (1973; 253 PAGES; M/M)

John Ross was the son of a Cherokee mother and a white father. He grew up to be the chief of the Cherokee Nation and a trusted confidant of President Lincoln during the Civil War. In this re-creation of his life, Ross transforms a loosely knit group of tribes into a confederation, with a constitutional government and himself as elected chief. He provides Andrew Jackson with troops in the War of 1812. However, Jackson remembers the tragic results of earlier Cherokee raids in Tennessee. Once he becomes president, Jackson moves the Cherokees from Georgia to the West. Ross loses leadership for a time, then is elected chief again and marries an heiress from Philadelphia. During the Civil War, Ross serves Lincoln, while most Cherokees ally themselves with the South.

MACKINLAY KANTOR (1904–1977)
Andersonville (1956; 753 PAGES; D/D)

Andersonville Prison in Sumter County, Georgia, became the scene of one of the most horrible episodes on either side during the Civil War. Over the course of fourteen months, 50,000 prisoners died there. The construction, administration, occupation, and supervision of the prison form the basis of this Pulitzer Prize–winning novel. A central character is Ira Claffey, on whose doorstep the prison is built. Harrell Elkins, a Confederate Army veteran, tries to lessen the suffering, as do many of the surrounding Southerners. Supervisor of the prison, Confederate General Winder, and the jailer, Henry Wirz, turn their backs on attempts to help. The Confederate government refuses to offer a prisoner exchange, and 14,000 of the prisoners choose to die instead of taking an oath to the South. Once the war ended, Henry Wirz became the only southern officer tried and executed for war crimes.

HAROLD KEITH (1903–)
Komantcia (1965; 296 PAGES; M/M)

Komantcia opens in 1865, when the Comanche Indians are at the height of their power in northern Mexico and the American Southwest. Pedro is a young Spanish aristocrat living on his uncle's ranch in northern Mexico. A brutal Comanche raid results in death for his mother and uncle and capture for himself and his brother. Despite fierce resistance, Pedro gradually adapts to Indian life, learns all of the customs, goes on raids, and becomes an expert horse thief. There was a real Pedro, who eventually returned to his former life.

HAROLD KEITH (1903–)
Rifles for Watie (1957; ABOUT 331 PAGES; M/M)

Kansas and Missouri played a large role in pre-Civil-War politics as the nation struggled to decide which state would be free and which slave. However, the actual wartime activity in these two states, Arkansas, and what is now Oklahoma is a lesser-known story. Against this backdrop, Jeff Bussey's story develops from 1861 to 1865. He lives in Linn County, Kansas, and once the secession takes place he joins the Union Army. Over the next four years, Jeff becomes acquainted with the role the Cherokee Nation plays in the war, becomes a Union scout behind Confederate lines, fights in battles all over the territory, and learns how all parties feel about the war.

THOMAS KENEALLY (1935–)
Confederates (1979; 421 PAGES; D/D)

Four stories run concurrently in this view of the Civil War from the southern side. In 1862, Usaph Bumpass is a member of the Shenandoah Volunteers. A Virginia farm boy, he is one of the thousands of ordinary Southern boys pressed into service. While away, his young wife must cope on her own. She is in strange land because her home is in the Carolinas. On the other hand, widow Dora Whipple is an efficient hospital matron who likes her job as a spy and becomes involved with a British journalist. Finally, there is all the horror and drama of the war itself—which, for the principal characters, climaxes in the Second Battle of Antietam.

WILLIAM KENNEDY (1928–)
Quinn's Book (1988; 289 PAGES; D/D)

Fourteen-year-old orphan Daniel Quinn's life changes forever in December 1849. This is the day Magdalena Colon drowns in Albany's Hudson River—and later comes back to life. Daniel helps move the body of the "dead" courtesan to the home of her wealthy friend. The friend is a widow with an impressive family history and important professional contacts. Through this association, Daniel embarks on a life of adventure and intrigue, eventually landing a job as a reporter for the *Albany Chronicle*. He becomes involved with and writes about many history-making events of the day, including the Underground Railroad, struggles for power among immigrant Americans, political conspiracies, draft riots, and the Civil War.

JOAN KING (1930–)
Impressionist (1983; 311 PAGES; D/D)

Mary Cassatt was an American artist whose fame and reputation were recognized by the French Impressionists, the French government, and eventually Americans. Many of her paintings are displayed today at the Musée d'Orsay in Paris. Born in 1861 in Philadelphia to wealthy parents, Cassatt wants to go to art school and to be an artist. Such an ambition is not suitable for a woman; however, thinking they will satisfy a temporary whim, Cassatt's parents allow her to go to school. Cassatt then goes to Europe, and finally to Paris, where she becomes acquainted with Impressionist painters of the day: Monet, Renoir, Gauguin, and especially Degas, who becomes a major influence. Cassatt, who never married, is known for her portraits of mothers and children.

FLETCHER KNEBEL (1911–1993) AND CHARLES W. BAILEY II (1929–)
Seven Days in May (1962; 341 PAGES; D/D)

This novel opens with President Dwight D. Eisenhower's 1961 warning of the possibility of a government takeover by the military-industrial complex. Published in 1962, the novel is set in futuristic 1974. The story centers around differences of opinion between civilian and military leaders regarding U.S. policies toward Russia. Colonel Martin Casey is director of the Joint Staff, a select group of officers responsible to the Joint Chiefs of Staff. Casey becomes suspicious of the activities of General Jim Scott, Chairman of the Joint Chiefs. Casey is convinced that Scott is planning a takeover of the government; he takes his suspicions to the president, Jordan Lyman. Dubious at first, Lyman investigates Casey's information. He finds that there is a planned takeover and that it is to occur shortly. The intelligence and patriotism of Colonel Casey are pitted against the logic and methods used in planning the military takeover, which have disturbing implications.

JACKIE FRENCH KOLLER (1948–)
Nothing to Fear (1991; 279 PAGES; M/M)

In New York City, young Danny Garvey and his Irish immigrant family eke out an existence during the Great Depression which gripped 1930's America. Danny shines shoes while his mother takes in laundry. His father leaves New York seeking work elsewhere. The Garveys' situation is not unique; everyone else is suffering, too. Sadie, an African-American maid, frets over bank closures and the possible loss of her life savings; Hank, a bankrupt farmer from Oklahoma, comes to the Garveys' building looking for his brother—only to find the brother has been evicted; friends and neighbors go hungry and work is increasingly hard to get. When Danny finds out that his father has died searching for work, his world nearly collapses. Only their faith in family, God, and newly elected President Franklin Roosevelt keep the Garveys striving to live through the Great Depression. Nonstandard English is used in both the narrative and dialogue.

JACKIE FRENCH KOLLER (1948–)
The Primrose Way (1992; 261 PAGES; M/M)

In 1633, sixteen-year-old Rebekah sails from England to join her father in a newly formed Puritan settlement in America. Conditions are primitive beyond Rebekah's imaginings, but she quickly adjusts. She has more difficulty with the attitudes of her fellow Puritans toward the Pawtucket Indians of Massachusetts, who are viewed as pagans and savages. Rebekah becomes fluent in the native language and thus learns a great deal. Knowledge and respect make her compassionate toward the natives, and for this she is punished by the Puritan settlers. Sickened by their treatment of the natives, Rebekah leaves the Puritan settlement to live with the tribal holy man Mishannock, with whom she has fallen in love. This story examines the righteous intolerance of the Puritans, who see no incongruity between their lack of respect and tolerance for native tribes and their spiritual beliefs.

NORA BENJAMIN KUBIE (1899–1988)
Joel (1952; 207 PAGES; M/M)

Young Jewish refugee Joel Davidov comes to America in 1775, seeking refuge from the persecution he has known in his native land of Warsaw, Poland. When political tensions burst into violence, Joel at first refuses to take sides in the conflict between the Americans and British. However, he is soon unjustly imprisoned by the British; this imprisonment gives him time to read Thomas Paine and hear about Nathan Hale. Inspired, Joel joins the colonists and fights with the Minutemen in New York and Connecticut. A romance with a Christian girl broadens his knowledge and perspective. By the end of the novel, Joel realizes what it is like to be both Jewish and American and loyal to democratic ideals.

EVELYN SIBLEY LAMPMAN (1907–1980)
Cayuse Courage (1970; 181 PAGES; E/E)

This novel tells the story of the "Whitman Massacre" of 1848 (an actual event). Samuel Little-Pony is a Cayuse Indian in the Oregon Territory. On a buffalo hunt, he dives into a swimming pool and an old trap closes on his hand. When the tribe's medicine man fails to cure him, Samuel is taken to a nearby white mission, where Dr. Marcus Whitman amputates his arm. Samuel stays at the mission for a time, then goes back to his village, although now he can never be a warrior. The Native-American frustration about continued white settlement eventually leads to an attack on the mission, the massacre of many, and the taking of prisoners.

EVELYN SIBLEY LAMPMAN (1907–1980)
Tree Wagon (1953; 244 PAGES; E/E)

In 1847, a wagon train leaving Iowa begins one of the more unusual trips west. Henderson Luelling, his wife, and their eight children, along with two other families, load a wagon with seven hundred fruit trees and berry bushes and leave for the West Coast. Three hundred and fifty survive—the first grafted fruit trees in Oregon. Based on this true event, the novel centers on the experiences of young Seenie Luelling and Peter Hockett. Although the children have exciting adventures, the journey is a serious one, with hardships for all as well as determination to bring new life into the West.

EVELYN SIBLEY LAMPMAN (1907–1980)
Wheels West (1965; 219 PAGES; E/E)

The real Tabitha Brown made the trek west to Oregon in the 1840's when she was well past sixty. Based on family histories, this novel re-creates Tabitha's journey west with her children and grandchildren. Week after week, they ride in a wagon train, slowing down only as necessary to deal with Native Americans, illness, weather, and hunger. Grandma (Tabitha) Brown proves to be the strongest and most resolute in the family. Once in Oregon, she continues to work hard in the settlement of the new community. Tabitha becomes one of the promoters of Tuelatin Academy, which later became Pacific University in Forest Grove, Oregon.

ROSE WILDER LANE (1887–1968)
Young Pioneers (1933; ABOUT 115 PAGES; E/E)

In the 1850's on the South Dakota frontier—one of the roughest areas in American territory—young David and Molly face the struggle to keep a farm going in harsh surroundings. Shaken by winter, insect plague, and Native-American threats, David decides to find work—even though it means leaving his wife and baby son. Molly is determined to keep the claim to the farm and land by staying in the dugout home David builds. Facing severe winter weather, dying cattle, and hungry wolves, Molly endures a brutal test of survival.

KATHRYN LASKY (1944–)
Beyond the Divide (1983; 250 PAGES; M/M)

In an unusual twist on the usual narratives of American pioneer life, the author creates an Amish father and daughter, Will and Meribah Simon, who leave their close-knit but rigid community in Pennsylvania to join the trek toward gold in California in 1849. In Missouri, the Simons join a group of migrants from different backgrounds. What begins as an adventurous journey soon turns into a brutal test of survival as Meribah's father falls ill, and the two are abandoned on the trail as winter begins. This is not only a pioneer tale, but an exploration of Amish life and the relationship between father and daughter. In addition, Meribah meets American Indians from the last North-American tribe to live freely (who were, unfortunately, eventually killed off in the last part of the nineteenth century).

JEAN LEE LATHAM (1902–)
Carry On, Mr. Bowditch (1955; 250 PAGES; M/M)

In 1779, the Revolutionary War still rages on and Nat Bowditch is only six years old. He and his family are about to move back to Salem, Massachusetts, hoping that their father's bad luck as a seaman (who has lost his ship) will change. From this opening, the story focuses on Nat as he grows up; we learn that he is an intelligent boy with many skills and talents. Nat spends a nine-year period as an indentured apprentice on a ship. (During this period, indentured servants—though oppressed—often learned a trade from their bondage.) Once free, Nat signs on as a seaman and sails the Caribbean and the Atlantic. He learns navigation and teaches it, soon realizing that good navigation is essential to avoid the high loss of ships in bad weather. Eventually, Nat becomes a captain and finds his true place in life in the new nation.

JEAN LEE LATHAM (1902–)
This Dear-Bought Land (1957; 246 PAGES; M/E)

The story opens with fifteen-year-old David Warren, born to live the life of a gentleman in England. Yet David desperately wants to sail with his father to Virginia with the New London Company in 1607. Upon his father's death, David sails to the New World alone. On board ship, he is challenged by Captain John Smith to be a tough seaman. David meets the challenge. The story focuses on Captain Smith, who faces challenges of his own. Nearly losing his ship to a planned mutiny, Captain Smith prevails—and goes on to become the sole leader of the infant colony of Jamestown, Virginia. Water and food shortages, a harsh environment, and hostile Native Americans threaten the town. Condemned to death by Chief Powhatan, Smith is saved by the Chief's daughter, Pocahontas. With most of the colonists dead or dying, and English supplies and men slow to arrive, the settlers prepare to return to England. Intercepting a ship bound for America, the colonists return to rebuild and maintain the first permanent English colony in America.

ISABELLE LAWRENCE
Drumbeats in Williamsburg (1965; 213 PAGES; M/M)

In 1781, after six years of Revolutionary War activities, the residents of Williamsburg (capital of Virginia) have become used to many military movements in and around the city. Twelve-year-old Andrew Small becomes involved in what will become the climax of the war—and its end—at Yorktown, Virginia. Andrew becomes a drummer boy. In this post, he crosses paths with General Washington, General Lafayette, and Lord Cornwallis. Because of a young boy's desertion from British forces, Andrew is able to wear his uniform and slip across the British lines more than once as he performs valuable service for the young nation.

WILLIAM J. LEDERER (1912–   ) AND EUGENE BURDICK (1918–1965)
The Ugly American (1958; 259 PAGES; M/M)

This book produced a great reaction when it was first published; its ideas are still not outdated. Not exactly a novel, this is a series of fictional stories linked by common themes. The setting is Southeast Asia in the 1950's. The stories concern several Americans in various countries—mythical and real—who mostly represent America badly. The characters include an American ambassador, a Navy captain, a Catholic priest, an engineer, a Russian ambassador, American businessmen, and others. The themes focus on the American tendency to reward individuals with ambassadors' posts as political gifts, and the inability of U.S. ambassadors and most foreign-service officers to speak host countries' languages, or to learn about their cultures.

WILLIAM J. LEDERER (1912–   ) AND EUGENE BURDICK (1918–1965)
Sarkhan (1965; 307 PAGES; M/M)

In *Sarkhan,* as in *The Ugly American,* Lederer and Burdick express their point of view about United States policy in Southeast Asia through the story of a country called Sarkhan. Sarkhan's King Diad is about to abdicate his throne; the plot develops from this premise. The king's son, Lin, a scholar and political neutral, prepares to ascend the throne. A fisherman named Tue has orders from his Communist bosses in Hanoi, Vietnam, to disrupt events. The U.S. places faith in a "strongman," General Hajn. Two Americans in Sarkhan, a businessman and a scholar, watch the situation evolve. In Washington, the president and members of the Cabinet prepare both political and military responses to developing events.

HARPER LEE (1926–)
To Kill a Mockingbird (1960; 255 PAGES; M/M)

This is a classic novel about racism and single parenthood in the Depression era. Eight-year-old Scout and her older brother, Jem, are being raised in a small Alabama town in the 1930's by their widowed father and an African-American housekeeper. Atticus Finch is an attorney and a father with a firm grasp of human failings and a deep respect for people of any race, social class, or lifestyle. His earnest defense of a black man wrongly accused of raping a white woman creates a town crisis—and a vendetta against his family. Through the guidance and perception of Atticus, Scout and Jem grow to become more compassionate toward their neighbors, and to fight human injustice in any form.

LOIS LENSKI (1893–1974)
Indian Captive: A Story of Mary Jemison (1941; 270 PAGES; M/M)

In the early days of pioneer settlement in America, white children were often captured by Native Americans. One of the better-known actual examples was Mary Jemison, who was taken from her home in eastern Pennsylvania in 1758 and eventually settled in a Seneca village in western New York. Mary did have opportunities to return to white society over the next several years. However, she chose to remain with the tribe, and lived on the Genesee River until she died at the age of ninety in 1833. The novel woven around Jemison's story gives details of everyday Seneca life; the changes brought by white settlers; and the conflicts among the settlers, French, British, and Native Americans.

SONIA LEVITIN
Roanoke: A Novel of the Lost Colony (1973; 206 PAGES; M/M)

One of the enduring mysteries of American history is the unknown fate of the colony that settled on Roanoke Island (off the coast of present-day North Carolina) in 1585. The narrator of this account is the fictional character of William Wythers, a runaway sixteen-year-old apprentice. William joins the emigrants leaving England for Virginia, and embarks on a long ocean voyage. Once in the island colony, he and the settlers adjust to a harsh life and endure the hardships of winter. William becomes attached to the land and to the Native Americans, who regard the land with respect. The author bases William's story on an actual settler's written account. In the end, the settlers of the colony vanish; the author imagines their fate.

SINCLAIR LEWIS (1885–1951)
Elmer Gantry (1927; ABOUT 432 PAGES; D/D)

Shallow religious leaders have never been in short supply. In the early 1900's, Elmer Gantry attends a religious college in Kansas with the belief that he will become a wealthy lawyer one day. Hearty and hale but obnoxious, Elmer is an athlete and "big man on campus," never realizing that he is actually unpopular and considered a bully. Rowdy and irreverent, Elmer finds that his shallow charm appeals to religious zealots seeking a charismatic leader. From a small midwestern church to the vastness of a New York City pulpit, Elmer plies his charms—and often convinces himself of his righteousness and religious conviction. Seldom along his journey to fame and personal wealth does his hypocrisy catch up with him. Others who come into contact with him are less fortunate, and are often destroyed by his hold on politicians, businessmen, and his dutiful flock.

SINCLAIR LEWIS (1885–1951)
Arrowsmith (1925; ABOUT 327 PAGES; M/M)

Martin Arrowsmith, a fourteen-year-old boy in the Midwest, is an apprentice to a village doctor who has had little medical training. The doctor suggests that Martin become a licensed physician. This Martin does by going to school in New York and becoming an earnest student of an eccentric professor. Martin dislikes what he perceives to be an unfair university administration; he flees to become a country doctor, even though he prefers research. Tempted throughout his professional life by wealth and power, Martin comes to see that medicines which could be used to help people are used by labs and doctors to obtain huge profits. Although he succumbs occasionally to temptation, Martin remains true to his principles.

SINCLAIR LEWIS (1885–1951)
Babbitt (1922; ABOUT 244 PAGES; M/M)

In the 1920's, George Babbitt is a successful real-estate businessman in Zenith, New York. Married, and with children, a suburban house, and membership in all the right clubs, he is the best example of the "hale and hearty" American businessman. But Babbitt has problems. While ostensibly a devoted husband and father, George has an affair, and secretly socializes with a "fast" crowd. Wanting to think himself broadminded and socially liberal, George nonetheless finds himself cleaving to the conservative civic leaders in the community. In short, George is a hypocrite, proclaiming to be an example of the accepted norms of society, but actually leading a life that undermines and manipulates those norms.

SINCLAIR LEWIS (1885–1951)
Main Street (1920; ABOUT 335 PAGES; M/M)

Main Street is a cynical look at small-town America. Carol Milford, an attractive, sensitive, and intelligent young woman in 1920's Minneapolis, yearns for a more meaningful life. Uninterested in what she perceives to be the dreary lot of married women, Carol spurns the men who wish to court her. She then meets Dr. Will Kennicott, from the small town of Gopher Prairie. Portraying a picturesque village in need of someone of her superior qualities, the older, seemingly sensitive country doctor persuades Carol to marry him and move to his town. Carol unwittingly subjects herself to the intolerant citizenry of Gopher Prairie. Trying to bring "culture" to the town, she succeeds only in becoming an object of criticism. Carol resigns herself to a life of small tasks well done, larger issues left unresolved, and yearnings left unfulfilled.

ATHENA V. LORD (1932–)
A Spirit to Ride the Whirlwind (1981; 197 PAGES; M/M)

Lowell, Massachusetts, the setting for this novel, was the first planned factory town in the United States. It reflected a significant chapter in the change from farming to industrial America. The new textile mills attracted a new work force: women. Because men in the 1820's looked down on factory work and were still busily laying claims to land, women became the predominant work force in the New England textile mills. As *A Spirit to Ride the Whirlwind* begins, twelve-year-old Binnie Howe lives with her mother in a rooming house for mill workers. To make more money, Binnie is allowed to take an unskilled job in the mill. She finds the conditions severe. When wages are cut, she is caught between her desire to do right and protest and the necessity to protect her family. The seeds of union activity and women's rights groups can be found in this place and time period.

MARY E. LYONS
Letters from a Slave Girl: The Story of Harriet Jacobs (1992; 126 PAGES; M/M)

Based on an autobiography of Harriet Jacobs, a North Carolina slave, this story spans the period from 1825 to 1897. Born into slavery, Harriet nonetheless can read and write—skills normally denied to slaves. She keeps a journal in order to express the thoughts and frustrations that she dares not voice. Sexually harassed by a white master, Harriet plots escape to the North and freedom. She spends seven years of her young life hidden in the garret of a conspirator's home before her journey north begins. During her long life, Harriet has children, becomes an activist in the antislavery movement, and publishes her autobiography. Unlike most slave accounts, which were written by males, Harriet's published works were considered somewhat scandalous, since she details life for a female slave—including the sexual nature of the relationships forced on black women by white men. The book has a letter format and contains a considerable amount of dialect.

JOHN P. MARQUAND (1893–1960)
The Late George Apley (1937; 351 PAGES; D/D)

This is a critical look at Boston life from 1866 to 1933. George Apley lives in Boston in an era of war recovery, prosperity, high manners, relative security, and the arrival of the United States as a power on the world scene. The story, written by a biographer friend of the family, is told in memoir form. The memoirs not only recount the events of the fictitious Apley's life, but also present the general mood of the times. Apley is a Boston gentleman who lives his whole life in a narrow geographical area and a narrow social world. Boston life is defined by people's homes, schooling, associates, and occupation. Marquand won a Pulitzer Prize for this novel.

F. VANWYCK MASON (1901–1978)
Armored Giants (1980; 334 PAGES; M/M)

One of the key events of the Civil War—as well as a significant step in the technology of warfare—was the March 1862 battle between the Union ship *Monitor* and the Confederate ship *Merrimac* at Hampton Roads, Virginia. This first battle of ironclad ships is the central idea of the novel, which begins in 1861 in the midst of Lincoln's blockade of southern ports. A cast of both Northerners and Southerners are involved in the building and the battle of the ships: an Irishman; a young woman with a secret past; a British war correspondent; a Frenchwoman who is a spy; the central character, a Union Navy lieutenant who volunteers to go behind Confederate lines to learn about the new ship; and his fiancée, a Southerner. Mason wrote over 60 historical novels; this is the last one.

F. VANWYCK MASON (1901–1978)
Trumpets Sound No More (1975; 294 PAGES; M/M)

Trumpets Sound No More is about the South's struggle to survive and rebuild after the Civil War ended at Appomattox in April 1865. The story is set in a South that has no law and no civil government except in well-garrisoned federal strongholds. Most businesses, banks, communications, and transportation do not exist. Into this chaos steps Rodney Tilt, a former colonel in the Virginia Cavalry. Discharged, he gathers a group of men to return to his home in western Virginia. The journey is one of danger because of Union patrols and outlaws. When Tilt reaches his home, he is astonished to find that the family's mine, farmlands, and all sources of income have been destroyed. With the help of a seafaring friend, Tilt plans an expedition along the Mexican coast to recover a chest of gold—and, he hopes, to recover the means for a new start.

ROBERT M. MCCLUNG (1916–   )
Hugh Glass, Mountain Man (1990; 151 PAGES; E/E)

This is the story of Hugh Glass, a real-life mountain man and trapper of the old West. In 1823, Glass is savagely attacked by a grizzly bear and is abandoned by his friends. Hovering near death for days, Glass survives by treating his own wounds and eating berries, rattlesnakes, and roots. Upon recovery, he sets out to find and kill the two men who left him to die alone. Finding them, he has a change of heart and forgives them. His generosity stems in part from his Quaker grandmother's teachings—and also from the knowledge that he, too, abandoned someone once, a kind and devoted American-Indian girl. In 1833, Glass is killed by Native Americans. A marker in South Dakota memorializes Glass's ordeal and his courage.

RUTHANNE LUM MCCUNN (1946–   )
Thousand Pieces of Gold (1981; 294 PAGES; M/M)

This biographical novel recounts the life of Lalu Nathoy, later known as Polly Bemis, an actual person who was born in China in the late 1800's. Living in a peasant village, on the constant edge of starvation and fear of bandits, Lalu is actually captured by bandits and shipped to America as a slave. She is auctioned off to a Chinese saloon keeper in an Idaho mining camp. Lalu eventually wins her freedom, runs her own boarding house, and homesteads acreage on the Idaho River of No Return. After her death in 1933, Lalu/Polly's life became the essence of legend.

WILLIAM P. MCGIVERN (1927–1982)
Soldiers of '44 (1979; 409 PAGES; D/D)

One of the last and greatest counteroffensive actions of any war was the German attack on the Ardennes Forest in Belgium in the winter of 1944. This German action and the American defense raged for nearly two weeks and was covered extensively by the American press, not least because it involved the well-known General George Patton. In his fictional account, the hero is Sergeant Buell ("Bull") Docker; the action is concentrated on his fifteen-man gun section. The twelve days of fighting are told as personal stories of fear and valor. Once the war is over, a tribunal of Army officers investigates the battle in an attempt to reconstruct the actual incidents.

ELOISE JARVIS MCGRAW (1915–)
Moccasin Trail (1952; 244 PAGES; M/M)

In 1844, runaway Jim Keath becomes a trapper in the Oregon Territory, where he is attacked by a bear and left for dead. Crow Indians rescue him, and he lives and learns with them for several years. One day, Jim returns to trapping and stumbles across a letter written by his brother years before. Jim finds his family and tries to put himself back into white society, while at the same time leading his sister and brother into the newly settled Willamette Valley in Oregon. This is a many-layered story of the conflict of two cultures, a boy growing up, a fight for survival, and pioneer settlement.

STEPHEN W. MEADER (1892–)
Boy with a Pack (1939; ABOUT 295 PAGES; M/M)

Meader wrote close to three dozen historical adventure novels. This one concerns seventeen-year-old Bill Crawford, who leaves New Hampshire in the financially depressed year of 1837. He sets out alone with a pack full of goods to sell as he moves west to the Ohio country—now a state, but still a frontier area. Bill crosses Vermont, New York State, and Pennsylvania, then moves into Ohio. Along the way, he meets a cross-section of typical characters of the period: a crooked horse dealer, a canal-boat captain, a Virginia slave catcher, a Quaker family, and a girl whom he will later meet again in Ohio. There is a stereotypical portrait of a young male slave whom Bill helps to escape.

STEPHEN W. MEADER (1892–)
Keep 'em Rolling (1967; 185 PAGES; E/E)

Oregon in the mid-nineteenth century represented a haven of the "good life." Sixteen-year-old Dave Marsh and his family are part of a wagon train that makes the long, dangerous journey to Oregon in the 1840's. During the trek, Dave makes a good friend of Jeff Barlow, who is a scout with the train. Jeff gives good advice on finding water, hunting buffalo, and dealing with the Native Americans. As Dave, his family, and Jeff make the journey, they encounter swollen rivers, empty plains, and forbidding mountains. They also struggle against disease, drought, and Native Americans. By journey's end, Dave has become a seasoned hunter and is ready to play his part in settling the lush Oregon land.

ENID LAMONTE MEADOWCRAFT (1898–1966)
By Secret Railway (1948; 272 PAGES; M/M)

The Underground Railroad would not have been successful without cooperation between whites and blacks. In Chicago in 1860, young David Morgan leaves school to find something more exciting to do. He finds a job on the waterfront and meets an African-American boy named Jim. The two boys form a solid and enduring friendship. This friendship later prompts David to travel far from home to find Jim, who has been kidnapped and taken to Missouri—a slave state. David and Jim become involved with the Underground Railroad in the desperate attempt to get Jim back to Illinois (a free state). The adventure ends with a meeting between President Lincoln and David.

ENID LAMONTE MEADOWCRAFT (1898–1966)
By Wagon and Flatboat (1938; ABOUT 163 PAGES; E/E)

Ohio was once the "West" to American settlers. In 1789, the Burd family decides to move out West to seek good land. Leaving Pennsylvania, Mr. and Mrs. Burd and the children (Jonathan, Andrew, and Sally) begin their journey in a Conestoga wagon. At York, they are joined by the Mathews family. At Pittsburgh, which consists of a few log cabins and stores, the family switches to a flatboat. They also meet Mary Moore, who has been captured by Native Americans and then rescued. They all float down the Ohio River, encountering other pioneers and Native Americans along the way. At Losantiville (which eventually becomes Cincinnati), they disembark to make a home in the new frontier territory.

ENID LAMONTE MEADOWCRAFT (1898–1966)
The First Year (1943; 139 PAGES; E/E)

A simply told tale, *The First Year* recounts the early 1600's voyage of the *Mayflower* from England to the Massachusetts coast and the first year the new settlers spend in Plymouth Colony. The story is told mainly through the experiences of young Giles Hopkins, his mother and father, and the Brewster family. Governor Bradford, Miles Standish, and Squanto also play a part in the story. During the first year the settlers face many challenges—building cabins, finding food, adapting to the environment, withstanding the winter, and learning to deal with the Native Americans, some of whom are friendly and some of whom are not. Death stalks most of the Pilgrim families, but the first good harvest is celebrated by a Thanksgiving feast. New colonists arrive from England to join the Pilgrims before another winter sets in.

ENID LaMONTE MEADOWCRAFT (1898–1966)
We Were There at the Opening of the Erie Canal (1958; 179 PAGES; E/E)

Three faded letters written by a great-great aunt telling of her trip on the Erie Canal in 1827 prompted the author to create this story. Christopher, Kathy, Danny, and Peter Martin arrive in Albany, New York, to stay for a while with their Aunt Jane. Their father is completing medical training in England. Aunt Jane also has taken in an older boy, Tom, whose parents have died. Over the next year, the story focuses on the building and completion of the Erie Canal. Tom and then Christopher work on the canal from Albany to Lockport; they both see the canal's completion at Buffalo. When the children's father returns, he decides that the entire family should move west to Buffalo to participate in the new life the canal will bring.

JAMES A. MICHENER (1907–   )
Legacy (1987; 149 PAGES; E/M)

Many topics of historical concern are included in this relatively short novel. In 1985, Major Norm Starr is happy to be promoted to an appointment with the National Security Council in Washington, D.C. He is less happy to learn that his entire career could be in jeopardy, and that it depends on the testimony he must give to the Senate regarding his involvement with Nicaragua and the Contra opposition movement. Starr's lawyer, hoping to impress the Senate with Starr's patriot ancestry, instructs him to investigate the family history. Starr decides that he cannot in good conscience use his illustrious family to cloak himself in the American flag and escape scrutiny. He is instead reminded of the values that made his family great. Residing in the family tree are a Revolutionary War hero, a signer of the Constitution, a Supreme Court justice, a Civil War veteran, and a suffragette. Each of these and other ancestors are portrayed thoroughly; many topics of historical concern are included.

CHARLES K. MILLS
A Mighty Afternoon (1980; 181 PAGES; E/E)

Of enduring interest in American history is the Battle of the Little Bighorn in Montana on June 25, 1876, between General George Armstrong Custer and the Sioux. Custer's 7th Cavalry of 600 met 2,000 Sioux warriors and suffered the worst defeat of the American army at the hands of the Indians—indeed, perhaps the worst U.S. military defeat ever. In *A Mighty Afternoon*, Custer, his officers, his Indian scouts, and the men of the 7th Cavalry are brought to life in conversation and action between June 22 and June 28, 1876. The personalities, the course of the battle, and some reasons why the battle occurred as it did are main themes of the narrative.

MARGARET MITCHELL (1900–1949)
Gone with the Wind (1936; ABOUT 1019 PAGES; D/M)

Mitchell wrote only one novel, and this one earned a Pulitzer Prize. The now-familiar epic of southern plantation life before and during the Civil War burst upon the scene in 1936, and seems to have permanently etched on American minds this picture of the Georgian aristocratic class. Scarlett O'Hara and Rhett Butler are the main characters whose lives intertwine throughout the story. Beginning in 1861, the author describes the details of Tara plantation life at its height, the course of the Civil War, the battle in which Atlanta is burned, the ravaging of Tara and other plantations, and the attempts by the South to recover in the Reconstruction era. Despite its immense popularity, the novel should be read with an accompanying history of the period.

LOUISE MOERI (1924–)
Downwind (1984; 121 PAGES; E/E)

Disaster resulting from nuclear energy is the theme of this story. In a small town near Sacramento, California, families are gripped with fear by the possibility of a meltdown at a nearby nuclear power plant. Twelve-year-old Ephraim Dearborn and his family flee their home for safety. The roadways are crowded with panic-stricken motorists. The Dearborns are aided by kind and helpful strangers, but they are also terrorized by drunken men. Because of state tax cuts, there is no civil defense department—and, therefore, no strategic plans for emergencies. As the Dearborns and others struggle for an organized escape from danger, the pressing need for governmental responsibility to safeguard nuclear energy becomes frighteningly clear.

LOUISE MOERI (1924–)
Save Queen of Sheba (1981; 116 PAGES; E/E)

This is a tale of survival in rough country. On the Oregon Trail south of the Platte River in the early to mid-nineteenth century, Sioux Indians attack a wagon train of settlers. Young King David and his small sister, Queen of Sheba, survive. Wounded and left with the care of a six-year-old, King David sets out after other wagons ahead of them on the trail. King David has to find transport, provide food, secure shelter, comfort his sister, and find the tracks of the wagon train. At the same time, the Native-American threat still lurks nearby in the countryside.

YVETTE MOORE (1958–)
Freedom Songs (1991; 168 PAGES; E/E)

Fourteen-year-old Sheryl lives in Brooklyn, New York, in 1963. She is not prepared for the way she and her family are treated when they visit her grandmother in North Carolina. Although blacks are not treated as equals by whites in New York, the segregation practices of the South come as a rude shock. Her Uncle Pete is a Freedom Rider in North Carolina; he organizes protests and registers blacks to vote. When Sheryl returns to New York, she forms an organization to raise funds for the Freedom Riders down South. When Pete is murdered for his activism, Sheryl returns for his funeral. She participates in a peaceful protest which quickly turns ugly. Then she returns to New York more determined to fight racism.

WRIGHT MORRIS (1910–)
Plains Song: For Female Voices (1980; 229 PAGES; M/M)

Women have always been a diverse political group. From the 1920's to the 1970's, Cora Atkins presides over three generations of predominantly female families. Cora and her husband, Emerson, settle and farm on the Nebraska plains. Emerson's niece, Sharon, is the first of the Atkins to dislike farm life. She also dislikes the idea of marriage, deplores the lack of culture on the plains, and moves to Chicago to teach. Cora witnesses the results of progress on the farm as indoor plumbing, electricity, and the telephone arrive. Years later, Sharon returns to Nebraska for Cora's funeral. She is shocked by the change in her rural homeland—now a modern urban area. Now elderly, Sharon ponders the existence of two types of women: those who choose the seemingly endless historical tradition of marriage, and those—like herself—who believe marriage represents bondage and a dependent, primitive life.

MICHELE MURRAY (1933–1974)
The Crystal Nights (1973; 307 PAGES; M/M)

In 1938 and 1939, the United States was barely recovering from the Depression—and would not recover fully until its entrance into World War II. During those years, Elly Joseph and her family are living in a Connecticut farmhouse when the political problems in Europe touch their lives. Mr. Joseph's sister, Anna, and her daughter, Margot, have managed to escape the persecution of Jews in Germany and will now live with the Josephs. The adjustments required by both families and the eventual arrival of Michael, Anna's husband, from a prison camp are the main themes in the home setting. At school and in the community, the themes revolve around Elly and Margot's daily life in a period of rapid change, fear of strangers, and evidence of the Depression.

LIZA KETCHUM MURROW (1946–)
West Against the Wind (1987; 232 PAGES; E/M)

In the mid-nineteenth century, the quest for California gold lured many families into leaving their homes. This is the story of a young girl's experiences during the Gold Rush. In 1850, fourteen-year-old Abigail Parker is traveling west to California with her mother and brother. They are to join Abigail's father, who made the trip a year earlier from their home in Missouri. Abigail's father is in search of the gold said to be plentiful in California. Along the way, Abigail endures hunger, physical hardship, and personal danger. She also experiences the exhilarating sense of freedom that has come with the adventure of traveling in a wagon train. Abigail profits from the wisdom, judgment, and strength of her mother.

WALTER DEAN MYERS (1937–)
Fallen Angels (1988; 309 PAGES; M/M)

In 1967, during the Vietnam War, Richie Perry has just graduated from high school in Harlem and enlisted in the United States Army. With little prospect of a job or a college education, Richie sees the army as a way out of Harlem and a chance to see other parts of the world. Richie soon regrets his decision, when new buddies die around him in the seemingly meaningless political tug-of-war that envelops the tiny nation of Vietnam. Waiting fearfully in dark, wet trenches for signs of the enemy, Richie thinks of his mother and his younger brother, Kenny. While he wants Kenny to admire him, he also wants to avoid portraying killing as heroism to the impressionable boy. Wounded, hospitalized, and twice awarded the Purple Heart, Richie and his best buddy are finally sent home to the United States. Atypical of many war stories, *Fallen Angels* contains little sexism. The novel, which contains some adult language, concentrates on the soldiers' reaction to war and the reality of death rather than on minute descriptions of military tactics and maneuvers.

PHYLLIS REYNOLDS NAYLOR (1933–)
Walking Through the Dark (1976; 208 PAGES; M/M)

During the years 1931 to 1933, Ruth Wheeler and her family suffer through the early, shocking years of the Depression. Ruth's mother takes necessities to her former household helper, Annie Scoates, in a "Hooverville" near Chicago—one of the shantytowns which developed during this period. Within a year, Ruth's father loses his job, and the family begins a long, downhill slide into poverty. Ruth learns what it is like not to have good clothes, money for further schooling, and sufficient food. She also learns, in a period of growing up, which values are really important in life.

ANDRÉ NORTON (1912–)
Ride Proud, Rebel! (1961; ABOUT 213 PAGES; M/M)

This is the story of how two boys grow into adulthood during the Civil War, experiencing the conflicts between North and South in a border state. In 1863, Drew Rennie is sixteen. He leaves his grandfather's home in Kentucky to volunteer for the Confederate forces. Not only does he want to fight, but he also wants to escape his unhappy home life with his wealthy family. During the war he returns home to try to obtain horses for his company. Drew unintentionally inspires his second cousin Boyd Barrett to join the army. Drew and Boyd participate in General John Hunt Morgan's raids; eventually they are part of General N.B. Forrest's army in engagements throughout Kentucky, Tennessee, and Alabama. At the end of the war, Drew and Boyd return to Kentucky, where Drew finds out the truth about his family.

ROBERT C. O'BRIEN (1918?–1973)
Z for Zachariah (1975; 249 PAGES; M/M)

Many scientists and writers have projected what life would be like for survivors of a nuclear war. This writer imagines a valley with only two survivors. One is a teenager, Ann Burden, and the other is John Loomis, who joins her after searching the valley for days. He wears a safe-suit, something he developed in a lab to protect against radiation sickness. Not long after his arrival, however, he suffers a bout of the sickness. Once he is well, he begins to exhibit behavior that at first puzzles, then terrifies Ann, as she realizes that Loomis wants to keep her as a possession. How the two work out their relationship in a seemingly empty world is the theme of the story.

EDWIN O'CONNOR (1918–1968)
The Last Hurrah (1956; 424 PAGES; D/D)

This is a classic novel about one of the last of the old-style political bosses in the 1950's. Frank Skeffington, long-time Democratic mayor of a large city on the eastern seaboard, decides to run one more time. O'Connor subtly and slowly fleshes out the story of Skeffington's relationships with his ineffective son, his capable newspaper cartoonist nephew Adam, his wife Maeve, and a number of old political pals and enemies. The campaign unfolds step by step to its climax on election night, with Skeffington's defeat. The now-defeated mayor suffers a heart attack and slowly deteriorates, while Adam seeks explanations for his uncle's loss of the election. At the close of the novel, Skeffington dies, along with an era.

SCOTT O'DELL (1898–1989)
Carlota (1977; 153 PAGES; E/E)

Carlota takes place during the Mexican War, a dispute between the United States and Mexico over territory that includes California. In 1846 the ruling class of Mexican-owned California are people who have come to California from Spain to settle on ranches. They are divided in their loyalties. Some want to stay under Mexican rule, others want to be under American rule, and others do not care as long as they can keep their land. Carlota and her family are in the latter group, but they are caught up in the last days of the Mexican War and the changeover to American government. Carlota's father teaches her many skills that only boys usually learn, for his only son has died. Carlota uses these skills when she participates, along with her father, in the Battle of San Pasqual (an actual battle that took place December 6, 1846, near San Diego).

SCOTT O'DELL (1898–1989)
Island of the Blue Dolphins (1960; 184 PAGES; E/E)

Off the coast of California, southwest of Los Angeles, is the island of this story. In the early 1800's, a Russian sea captain and Aleutian Indian hunters arrive on the island and meet the resident tribe of Native Americans, the Ghales-at. Soon, a battle erupts and the tribe is weakened greatly. All but two are eventually taken off the island. These two, Karana and her brother, Ramo, remain. However, soon Ramo is killed by wild dogs. For the next eighteen years, Karana survives on the island by learning to deal with the wild dogs, avoid the Aleutian hunters, and live with nature. This story is based on true events.

SCOTT O'DELL (1898–1989)
Zia (1976; 179 PAGES; M/M)

Zia is a sequel to *Island of the Blue Dolphins,* which introduced the self-reliant Native-American woman Karana who lived on an island off California. In the late nineteenth century, Karana's niece Zia decides to move to the Santa Barbara mission with her younger brother Mando in order to be closer to her aunt. Zia hopes to reach Karana by sailing to the island on an old cast-up boat. Zia's journey to her aunt reflects her journey between the traditional world of her tribe and the modern world of the Spanish Catholic missionaries. How Zia copes with these two worlds, and what her aunt teaches her, are the main themes.

SCOTT O'DELL (1898–1989)
Sarah Bishop (1980; 184 PAGES; E/E)

American revolutionaries could be harsh on those not sharing their enthusiasm for freedom from England. After a raid by American revolutionary soldiers, Sarah Bishop is left alone on her British-sympathizing (or Tory) family's Long Island home. Her brother, Chad, joins the revolutionary side, which leaves her more isolated. Sarah must make a life of her own in dangerous times. This life leads her into the city of New York, into a British prison, and finally into the wilderness (present-day Westchester County), where she learns much about nature, Indian ways, and herself.

SCOTT O'DELL (1898–1989)
Sing Down the Moon (1970; 134 PAGES; E/E)

Sing Down the Moon takes place in the last two years of the Civil War (1863–1865), when the Navajo Indians of the Southwest are suffering through two of their most tragic years. A young Navajo girl, Bright Morning, experiences the events of those years. First, she is captured by Spanish slave catchers and sold to a Spanish family. Escaping from them, Bright Morning returns to her home. But soon the American army is on the march, burning crops, killing livestock, and forcing thousands of Navajos to walk several hundred miles to a new location. Bright Morning manages to escape from here, too. Eventually she and her husband, Tall Boy, move to a new place with new hope.

SCOTT O'DELL (1898–1989)
Streams to the River, River to the Sea (1986; 191 PAGES; E/E)

The Shoshone Indian woman Sacagawea has long captured the imaginations of those interested in the early 1800's Lewis and Clark expeditions. These expeditions ranged from St. Louis to the Pacific and back by way of the Missouri, Columbia, and Yellowstone rivers. O'Dell has constructed a novel that first focuses on Sacagawea's life before meeting Lewis and Clark. A Frenchman named Toussaint Charbonneau wins her in a game from a tribe called the Minnetarees, who captured her as a young girl. Charbonneau then marries Sacagawea. Lewis and Clark hire Charbonneau and Sacagawea to act as guides; she will also serve as interpreter. Sacagawea carries her infant son on the two-year journey from 1804 to 1806. She also suffers from the cruelty of her husband. At the end of the expedition, she escapes to return to her people. The real Sacagawea lived to be 98 years old and died in 1884.

Scott O'Dell (1898–1989) and Elizabeth Hall (1929–)
Thunder Rolling in the Mountains (1992; 126 pages; e/m)

In 1877, a young woman, Sound of Running Feet, is forced to move with her Nez Percé tribe from their homeland in Idaho. Nez Percé is the name given to the tribe by the whites. The tribe's real name is Ne-Mee-poo, or the Real People. Chief Joseph, Sound of Running Feet's father, believes in making peace with the whites, but the U.S. Army soldiers make peace impossible. The Ne-Mee-poo stand off army attacks as they flee toward Canada and the safety of Chief Sitting Bull's camp. Eventually, the Native Americans are outnumbered and defeated; they succumb to the fallen Chief Joseph's pledge—"I will fight no more forever."

Katherine Paterson (1932–)
Lyddie (1991; 182 pages; m/m)

Factory work for women in the mid-nineteenth century represented both freedom and bondage. The wages of two dollars or more a week was good money, but twelve- and fourteen-hour workdays were common. Into this life steps Lyddie Worthen, a farm girl from Vermont. Her father has deserted the family. Her mother has become an unstable religious fanatic who hires Lyddie and her brother out, then takes Lyddie's two younger sisters off to await the end of the world. Lyddie's dream is to earn money to reclaim the family farm. She runs away from the tavern job her mother has arranged and begins working in a mill in Lowell, Massachusetts. Lyddie unjustly loses her mill job because of a lecherous and vindictive boss. The farm has already been sold, and Lyddie is offered marriage by the new owner. She decides instead to attend the progressive Oberlin College in Ohio and achieve the independence so long denied her.

Robert Newton Peck (1928–)
Arly (1989; 150 pages; e/e)

Rural Florida in pre-Depression America had a large population of nearly destitute fruit and vegetable pickers. In 1927, eleven-year-old Arly Poole and his father, Dan, live in a rough shack and barely eke out an existence. Although they work long days at backbreaking labor, they are perpetually in debt for rent and food to Captain Tant, the boss of Jailtown. Arly's narrow and meager world is suddenly brightened by the arrival of a "famous lady," Miss Binnie Hoe. Miss Hoe is a schoolteacher and not really famous, but she is part of President Coolidge's plan to bring education to remote areas of the country. Dan Poole is her most ardent supporter, for he wants a better life for Arly than the circle of poverty they have always known. Miss Hoe illuminates the Pooles' world and Arly soon becomes her star pupil. Captain Tant makes it known that no picker in debt to him will ever leave Jailtown, but Miss Hoe has better aspirations for Arly.

ANNE PELLOWSKI (1933–)
First Farm in the Valley: Anna's Story (1982; 177 PAGES; E/E)
Winding Valley Farm: Annie's Story (1982; 183 PAGES; E/E)
Stairstep Farm: Anna Rose's Story (1981; 166 PAGES; E/E)
Willow Wind Farm: Betsy's Story (1981; 164 PAGES; E/E)

A series of four novels traces four generations of a Polish-American family on Wisconsin farmland beginning in 1876. Starting with first-generation parents who speak only Polish and whose children do not speak English until they enter school, the series ends in the 1960's. Throughout the generations, the family experiences changes in farm technology and family continuity. A family tree and Polish pronunciation guide are provided.

ANN PETRY (1908–)
Tituba of Salem Village (1964; 254 PAGES; M/M)

Two themes dominate this story: the personal history of a slave in colonial times and the hysteria surrounding the Salem witch trials in Massachusetts in the 1690's. One of the actual accused women is Tituba, who has come from Barbados. Being black, a slave, female, non-Christian, and more intelligent than others around her makes Tituba a prime suspect as a witch. The plot develops as suspicion and "evidence" accumulate against Tituba, who is finally brought to trial with other women. Tituba confesses—an act which often brought acquittal or jail (denial often resulted in conviction or death). Tituba goes to jail, later is bought by another master, and lives out her life in Boston.

JAYNE PETTIT
My Name Is San Ho (1992; 149 PAGES; E/E)

A small child named San Ho and his mother are living in a small village near Saigon, South Vietnam, when the Vietnam War breaks out. By 1973, the village is ruined by constant battles between the Communists and the Americans. Like many thousands of Vietnamese, San Ho and his mother flee first to Saigon, then to the United States, to escape the Communist takeover of their country. In Philadelphia, San Ho, his mother, and her new husband (a young American Marine) create a good life in spite of the prejudice of some of their neighbors. San Ho learns to enjoy American life, yet still mourns the tragedy which has befallen his native land. The book contains a brief introductory explanation of the history of Vietnam and a strong emphasis on Vietnamese culture.

ADRIENNE RICHARD (1921–)
Pistol (1969; 242 PAGES; M/M)

"Pistol" becomes Billy Catlett's nickname when he signs on at age fourteen to become a horse wrangler in Montana. He considers this the greatest day of his life, but soon the Depression comes—and brings with it a trail of destruction. Billy's father loses his job, the finance company repossesses all they own, and the family relocates to a tar-paper shack in a new town near a dam site. Billy decides to strike out on his own. On his way to coping with the Depression and growing up, he encounters such hazards as a prairie fire and a blizzard. The novel has a strong sense of time and place as well as much period detail.

CONRAD RICHTER (1890–1968)
The Light in the Forest (1953; ABOUT 179 PAGES; E/E)

For eleven years, since age four, John Butler has lived with the Delaware Indians in eastern Ohio as True Son. He considers himself a Native American. But suddenly, in 1765, a military expedition led by Colonel Bouquet comes through the area, and True Son is forcibly returned to his blood relatives in western Pennsylvania. He struggles to make the adjustment, leaving once to go back to the forest and life with the Delawares. However, in a momentary lapse, he betrays the Delawares to the whites. For this, he is cast out of the tribe and must return to the white civilization.

CONRAD RICHTER (1890–1968)
A Country of Strangers (1966; ABOUT 166 PAGES; E/E)

A sequel to *The Light in the Forest,* this novel introduces Stone Girl, who is fifteen and has lived with Native Americans since age four. Shortly before the American Revolution, Stone Girl leaves her home in eastern Ohio and sets out on a journey to find her white father, a Pennsylvania politician. Stone Girl has married early and takes with her a young son. When she arrives at her father's home, she receives a mixed reception. Her grandmother wants to accept her, but her father rejects her and her son. During the story, both Stone Girl's husband and son die. Eventually she must decide which way of life to choose.

CONRAD RICHTER (1890–1968)
The Trees (1940; ABOUT 302 PAGES; M/M)

Before being settled by the hardiest of American families in the late 1700's, land west of the Allegheny Mountains and north of the Ohio River was a primitive wilderness. Vast acres of trees, broken only by American-Indian trails, presented challenges and struggles to the families bent on settling here. Sayward Luckett belongs to such a family. With game gone from their Pennsylvania homeland, Sayward and her family journey to the rich land across the Ohio River. After Sayward's mother dies of hardship, her father presses Sayward to marry and raise the rest of the children. Eventually she marries Portius Wheeler, a rugged and taciturn man. Together they hack a home out of the dense forest. Dialect and slang are present.

CONRAD RICHTER (1890–1968)
The Fields (1946; 288 PAGES; M/M)

The Fields continues the story of Sayward Luckett, who has traveled with her family to the Ohio wilderness in the late 1700's. It is now the early 1800's, and Sayward is married to Portius Wheeler. A simple woman of fierce determination, Sayward guides and cares for her large family. While others give up the fight to clear the wilderness and decide to move into a nearby town, Sayward continues to clear the land. Portius teaches at the local school and dabbles in law and local politics. Eventually the trees are conquered, the land is planted, a good living is available, and more settlers move into the new state of Ohio. The once vast, forested wilderness is transformed into farmland and towns.

CONRAD RICHTER (1890–1968)
The Town (1950; ABOUT 286 PAGES; M/M)

This is the third in a trilogy of American pioneer-life novels centering on Ohio in the early and middle 1800's. *The Town* continues the story of Sayward Luckett Wheeler and her family in the new town of Americus. Chiefly told from the perspective of Chancey, one of Sayward's children, the novel follows Chancey from the age of about four into young adulthood and a career at the newspaper. The novel also follows the career of Chancey's father, who becomes a judge, and the lives of the rest of the family. Themes of importance in *The Town* are the hardships of pioneer life, the transition from the cleared forest to town life, and the struggle between generations—the older generation seeking to pass on the values of a traditional life to the younger generation, which must struggle with new conditions. Richter used Ohio historical documents to write this novel; it won a Pulitzer Prize.

CONRAD RICHTER (1890–1968)
The Sea of Grass (1937; ABOUT 146 PAGES; E/E)

A continuing current in the settlement of the American West in the second half of the nineteenth century was the rivalry—often violent—between rancher and settler or farmer. This novel shows how such rivalry affected one ranching family. James Brewton owns the largest ranch in Texas. He is challenged by newly arrived settlers, represented by a young, ambitious lawyer who wants to use the land in a different way. Also newly arriving from St. Louis is Brewton's intended wife, Lutie, who dislikes this sprawling, vast land. The conflict and the Brewtons' life develop over several years to form the heart of the story.

ANN RINALDI (1934–   )
In My Father's House (1993; 303 PAGES; M/M)

The first battle of the Civil War, the Battle of Bull Run, was fought on the property of Will McClean and his family in 1861 at Manassas, Virginia. To escape the war, the McCleans move to the quiet town of Appomattox, Virginia. Young Oscie, McClean's proud and contentious stepdaughter, is convinced that neither she nor the South will change because of the war with the North. The McCleans own slaves, but since they treat their slaves well, Oscie wrongly assumes that all Southerners do the same. She is rudely awakened to the reality that this is not so. She also comes to realize that even if slaves are treated well, they remain property to be dealt with at the whims of their owners. The ugliness of war contrasts unpleasantly with the glamour and gallantry of the soldiers. The war ends in 1865, and the South's surrender takes place—ironically—on the property of Will McClean and his family in Appomattox.

ANN RINALDI (1934–   )
The Last Silk Dress (1988; 344 PAGES; M/M)

The Last Silk Dress is based on an actual element of the Civil War—the South's use of a hot-air balloon to monitor Union forces. Fourteen-year-old Susan Chilmark's quarrelsome mother has raised Susan to be a southern belle. However, now her mother unjustly considers Susan a Yankee sympathizer. To prove her patriotism, Susan nurses Confederate soldiers. She also organizes a collection of silk dresses for use in making a balloon to spy on Union troops. Meanwhile, Susan discovers that her older brother, Lucien, is not the scoundrel he has been portrayed as by her parents. She also finds out that her stepfather has had an affair with a black slave. In the end, although the balloon is a success, Susan decides that the war is a futile one, and that both secession and slavery are wrong.

ANN RINALDI (1934–   )
A Ride into Morning (1991; 266 PAGES; M/M)

Tempe Wick lives on her family farm in New Jersey during the American Revolution. Her cousin Mary has been sent to live with Tempe, because Mary's family can no longer tolerate her overt activism as a Patriot. The Pennsylvania Line of the American Revolutionary Army has camped on Tempe's farm. As she sees the privation and hunger the soldiers endure, Tempe begins to lose sympathy with the revolutionary cause. It is Tempe's estranged brother, Henry (thought to be a lunatic), who brings her information that stirs her patriotism again. The biographies of the real Tempe Wick and her family are included in the afterword to this book.

ANN RINALDI (1934–   )
Wolf by the Ears (1991; 248 PAGES; M/M)

Thomas Jefferson owned many slaves on Monticello and other plantations. This novel is prefaced by a quote from Thomas Jefferson concerning slavery: "... we have the wolf by the ears, and we can neither hold him, nor safely let him go. Justice is on one scale, and self-preservation the other." One of Jefferson's slaves is Sally Hemings, half-sister to his deceased wife. Sally has a daughter, Harriet Hemings, who is about to reach the age when she will be set free by Jefferson. If Harriet accepts her freedom, she will have to leave Monticello and Virginia, as the law requires a freed slave to do. If she relinquishes her freedom and stays, she faces the prospect of being sold with the rest of Jefferson's property upon his death. The novel details many issues surrounding slavery, as well as the daily life of Monticello and the slaves who consider it home. A glossary explains terms used in the eighteenth and nineteenth centuries.

KENNETH ROBERTS (1885–1957)
Northwest Passage (1937; ABOUT 628 PAGES; D/D)

The lure of finding a northwest passage from the East to the West through North America fascinated explorers, who wanted a quicker way to reach the treasures of the Orient. Many died in the search for this route. With this as a continuing theme, the novel follows the life of young Langdon Towne, beginning in 1757 when he enters Harvard. He stays only two years, then joins Robert Rogers and a group of British Rangers on an expedition to the East. After Towne returns home, he spends time in London studying art in pursuit of his dream to be a painter. He meets Rogers again, and they return to North America in an attempt to find the passage—a trip that takes them on the major lakes and rivers.

Robert Skimin (1929–   )
Chikara! (1983; 541 pages; d/d)

Chikara! is a multigenerational saga spanning the early 1900's to the 1980's. Sataro Hoshi leaves Japan in 1907 for San Francisco, bringing with him his wife and one of their two sons. The Hoshi family amasses a fortune in America, but soon faces tragedy brought on by Sataro's involvement with bootlegging gangsters. His wife returns to Japan to be with the son they left behind, and Sataro remarries. He and his family incur more financial misfortune and suffer from racism and bigotry as war with Japan appears imminent. Returning to Japan, on old but once again prosperous man, Sataro, now widowed, seeks out his first wife. Together they die when Hiroshima is bombed by the Americans during World War II. The term *chikara* means power. Sought by Sataro when he first came to America in 1907, power is finally achieved not by him or his sons, but by his Japanese-born granddaughter, who becomes a Japan-based international power broker in electronics and banking. The novel contains sexual situations.

Gloria Skurzynski (1930–   )
Good-bye, Billy Radish (1992; 137 pages; e/m)

In 1917, as the United States enters World War I, young Hank Kerner is living in Canaan, Pennsylvania, a steel town. Most of the males over fourteen who are not off fighting in the war work in the steel mill. Hank's best friend, a Ukrainian immigrant named Bazyli Radichevych—dubbed Billy Radish—plans to work in the mill when he turns fourteen. The townspeople regard the wartime millworkers as heroes, and so does Billy. Hank is not so sure, even though his brother and father work in the mill. Hank considers the mill an evil place that kills, maims, and prematurely ages the workers. He decides to become a doctor after witnessing the birth of his nephew and seeing Billy stricken with a deadly influenza. A central question posed by this story of World War I America is what actually defines a hero—or, indeed, an American.

Gloria Skurzynski (1930–   )
The Tempering (1983; 178 pages; e/e)

In the early twentieth century, steel foundries provided jobs for entire communities. Andrew Carnegie was a founder of the steel industry. In his steel towns, he built libraries and pool halls and felt he was doing a great public service. In such a town in Pennsylvania, fifteen-year-old Karl Kerner plans to quit school and go to work in the steel mill. His new teacher, with whom he is in love, has other—musical—plans for his future. Finally, after coming to a better understanding of the dynamics and politics within the steel industry, Karl does decide to work in the mill, but as a manager rather than a laborer.

DORIS BUCHANAN SMITH (1934–)
Salted Lemons (1980; 233 PAGES; M/M)

Salted Lemons is about different kinds of discrimination suffered in America. Ten-year-old Darby Bannister has to move from Washington, D.C., to Atlanta, Georgia, in the middle of World War II. Moving is hard enough, but making friends is even tougher. The Georgians consider Darby a foreigner because she is a Yankee—from the North. However, others are in worse situations than Darby. Mr. Kaigler, who runs a grocery store, is from Germany. Yoko, who becomes Darby's friend, was born in the United States but looks different because of her Oriental heritage. The U.S. is at war with Germany and Japan, and it seems that the South is still fighting the North in the Civil War. Young Darby must figure all of this out in a confusing time.

BARBARA SMUCKER (1915–)
Runaway to Freedom: A Story of the Underground Railway (1978; 149 PAGES; E/E)

Almost nothing about slavery and the Civil War period arouses as must interest as the Underground Railroad. After escaping from slavery on a Mississippi plantation, twelve-year-old Julilly and her friend Liza run north toward Canada and freedom. Along the way, they receive help from both blacks and whites who act as "captains" at the various "station" stops. Many of the experiences of the girls (who disguise themselves as boys) are frightening, and they show great courage in their quest for freedom. Actual historical figures and incidents enter the story.

VIRGINIA DRIVING HAWK SNEVE (1933–)
Betrayed (1974; 109 PAGES; E/E)

The Sioux, or Dakota Indians, were made to live on reservations set aside for them in Dakota Territory. They had been promised money in return for their lands, but the United States government turned the money over to traders, who kept most of it. In 1862, the Santee—the most peaceful of the Sioux tribes—attack a white settlement in Minnesota and carry off many whites, including Sarah, her mother, sister, and neighbors. The Santee are near starvation and the kidnapping serves as their revenge against broken treaties. But other Native Americans of the Teton Sioux track down the Santee and their captives. This attack did occur in 1862, and many of the Santee were hanged.

RICHARD F. SNOW (1947–)
Freelon Starbird (1976; 206 PAGES; M/M)

This novel shows that not all soldiers signed up for battle out of patriotism during the American Revolution. In Philadelphia, one morning in 1776, Freelon Starbird wakes up after a drunken night. He finds that he and his friend Jib Grasshorn have signed up in the army to fight the British. Freelon relates his experiences as a soldier during the war. He is one of thousands of young men who find themselves basically untrained for military life in all respects: killing other soldiers, being uncomfortable, being sick or hurt, and being hungry. However, Freelon injects humor into his narrative—which is unusual with its antiwar, antihero, "accidental patriot" characteristics.

ROSE SOBOL (1931–)
Woman Chief (1976; 95 PAGES; E/E)

Based on a trapper's journal, *Woman Chief* gives a brief fictional account of a true story of the only known woman to become a chief of the Crow nation. In 1815, Lonesome Star is captured by Crow Indians in a raid on her tribe, the Gros Ventres of the Prairie. Raised by a Crow warrior, she soon reveals unusual abilities. Instead of learning to sew, pick berries, cook, plant, or be a craftswoman, Lonesome Star becomes a horsewoman, hunter, and warrior with no equal. Ranging near the Rocky Mountains, Woman Chief attracts many young male warriors as her followers. Woman Chief is killed on a peace mission to her native tribe, the Gros Ventres.

ELIZABETH GEORGE SPEARE (1908–)
Calico Captive (1975; 181 PAGES; M/M)

Early one morning in 1754, Indians raid the settlement of Charlestown, New Hampshire, and take captives to be ransomed. (The raid and capture were real events in the French and Indian Wars [1756–1763], which raged on the North American continent between the English and the French and their Indian allies. American colonists were caught up in what really was a global contest for supremacy between two empires.) Young Miriam Willard and her family, the captives, are the central characters in the drama of a journey northward to French Canada and Montreal, where they are to be sold to the French. Miriam and her family encounter the alien French culture in Montreal, and are later released to sail to England in a prisoner exchange. The real family on which the novel is based eventually returned to the colonies.

ELIZABETH GEORGE SPEARE (1908–)
The Prospering (1967; 368 PAGES; M/M)

In 1737, Ephraim Williams and his family come to Indian Town, a settlement in western Massachusetts Bay Province, to begin an experiment. Along with four other families, they hope to engage in cooperative living between Native Americans and whites. Through the fictional words of Elizabeth, one of the Williams's daughters, the novel describes the experiment and the evolution of the settlement into Stockbridge. Between 1737 and 1784, Elizabeth witnesses the growth of the colony into an important town, participates in the activities of an ambitious family, and watches the experiment fail when the Indians are forced to move west. Ephraim Williams was a real person; one of his sons founded Williams College. Puritan Jonathan Edwards's writings were completed during his ten years of missionary work in Stockbridge.

ELIZABETH GEORGE SPEARE (1908–)
The Sign of the Beaver (1983; 135 PAGES; E/E)

The Sign of the Beaver is based on incidences of Native Americans teaching settlers how to survive on the land. Thirteen-year-old Matt and his father have come from Massachusetts to Maine in 1768 to settle a claim. They build a cabin and plant crops; then Matt's father goes back to Massachusetts to bring the rest of the family. Matt is left alone to guard the cabin and tend the crops. However, a stranger comes by and steals the only rifle, which makes it nearly impossible to kill for food. Matt is helped through the rest of the summer and into the winter by a Beaver Indian boy, who teaches Matt how to survive and becomes his friend.

ELIZABETH GEORGE SPEARE (1908–)
The Witch of Blackbird Pond (1958; 249 PAGES; M/M)

This novel concerns the fear of witches, a phenomenon that was not unique to Salem, Massachusetts, in colonial times. As the story begins, Kit Tyler arrives in Wethersfield, Connecticut, in the spring of 1687, from Barbados. Brought up unconventionally in a wealthy family, Kit is now an orphan who will live in her aunt's Puritan household. Seeking air and space from the rounds of cleaning and scrubbing, Kit goes to the Meadows. There she meets Hannah, a lonely, bent figure who is regarded by the colonists as a witch. Kit also meets Prudence Cruff, a shy young girl, whom Kit teaches to read and write—against Prudence's parents' wishes. Then a mysterious illness strikes the children of the town. This begins a chain of events linking Hannah, Kit, and Prudence, who are accused of being witches.

ROBERT M. SPECTOR
Salt Water Guns (1970; 216 PAGES; E/E)

Fifteen-year-old Christopher McBride is a student at the Boston Latin School late in the Revolutionary War. Bored, restless, and eager to join the militia, Chris finds himself in constant trouble at school and in the town. His mother, who is at the point of despair, decides to allow Chris to be a cabin boy on a merchant ship. He is unhappy with this decision and has a poor attitude on first arriving at the ship. However, he soon finds out that the *Warrior*'s mission is to provide guns to the colonists along the Carolina and Georgia coasts. Chris also learns what responsibility, loyalty, and growing up really mean in a wartime period.

MARY Q. STEELE (1922–1992) AND WILLIAM O. STEELE (1917–1979)
The Eye in the Forest (1975; 134 PAGES; E/E)

The Adena people lived in Ohio, possibly from about 1000 B.C. to 100 A.D., and then mysteriously disappeared. They were named Adena because their burial mounds were discovered on the governor's estate, called Adena, near present-day Chillicothe, Ohio. From this slim outline and from artifacts, the author constructs a tale of an Adena youth, Kontu, who undertakes a long journey with some of his people to find the Sacred Eye. Kontu's priest-teacher leads the group on a perilous trip from Chillicothe through Kentucky and into Tennessee, where they hope to find the sacred place where their tribe originated.

WILLIAM O. STEELE (1917–1979)
Flaming Arrows (1957; 175 PAGES; E/E)

In the late 1700's, in Tennessee, the Chickamauga Indians are again threatening to attack settlers. Eleven-year-old Chad Rabun's family moves into one of the forts that have been built for settlers to use as walled defenses in case of Indian raids. The Rabuns share the fort with the Logan family and other families seeking protection. The Logans fall under suspicion because Mr. Logan has gone over to the Native-American side. As supplies and water dwindle, the other families consider making the Logans leave the fort. Then, Native Americans attack the fort, and young Josiah Logan fights as well as anyone. Chad must review how he thinks about other people and their behavior under extraordinary circumstances. The story includes a realistic depiction of how many settlers viewed Native Americans at the time and contains racist language.

WILLIAM O. STEELE (1917–1979)
The Lone Hunt (1956; 173 PAGES; E/E)

Yance Caywood lives on the Cumberland Plateau in northern Tennessee in 1810. He is only eleven years old, but he dreams of hunting buffalo—although there have not been any in the area for years. The buffalo, like most of the Native Americans, are moving west. On the farm, Yance does many chores for his mother; he and his brother, Pleas, have cared for her since their father died. One day, Yance gets his chance to hunt buffalo when tracks are spotted. He is allowed to go with the hunters. One by one, each of the hunters drops out as the weather worsens. Yance stays on alone, and accomplishes the work of an adult in both surviving and hunting.

WILLIAM O. STEELE (1917–1979)
The Man with the Silver Eyes (1976; 144 PAGES; E/E)

Talatu, a Cherokee Indian boy, lives with his great-uncle in Tennessee. One day, in 1780, his great-uncle tells Talatu he must go live and work for a year with a white trader named Shinn, who is a Quaker. Hating whites and not understanding Shinn's religion, which teaches living peacefully with all, Talatu reluctantly goes. Despite the Revolutionary War, Shinn tries to treat both British and colonists equally. Despite the fact that Native Americans have killed his family, Shinn treats Talatu with respect and kindness. At the end of the year, Talatu finds he no longer thinks or feels the same about himself or the whites.

WILLIAM O. STEELE (1917–1979)
The Perilous Road (1958; 182 PAGES; E/E)

Staying neutral during the Civil War, which was tearing the country and many families apart, is an attitude that Chris Brebson cannot understand. Yet his parents refuse to take sides—despite the presence of the war for two years all around their Tennessee mountain farm. Chris hates the Union troops, but his brother joins the Union army. Chris vows to join the Confederate army and, as an act of support, he reports the presence of a Union supply train coming up the valley. The full meaning of the war and how war affects people's behavior becomes apparent to Chris when he realizes that his brother might be in the supply train troops.

WILLIAM O. STEELE (1917–1979)
The Wilderness Tattoo (1972; 180 PAGES; E/E)

A Spaniard's camaraderie with Native Americans is the heart of this story. Seventeen-year-old Juan Ortiz, captured by Indians after being abandoned by his countrymen, learns to live as a native in sixteenth-century Florida. After many years of yearning to return to Spain, he becomes content with life among the Indians. Then, Hernando de Soto arrives with his expedition. Serving as de Soto's guide and interpreter, Juan explores the vast Floridian region. Juan finds he has much in common with the natives, whom he now considers his family. Thus, Juan does not share the Old World, Christian view of Native Americans as savage, dirty beasts, but rather as religious, spiritual human beings with a natural affinity for their homeland. Upon Juan's death, the Spanish explorers realize his overwhelming value as a guide and interpreter. As for Juan, he dies in a beautiful and majestic land he has come to love.

WILLIAM O. STEELE (1917–1979)
Trail Through Danger (1965; 173 PAGES; E/E)

Lafe Birdwell, at age eleven, is one of many young boys who grew up quickly in the pioneer days of the late 1700's. He is all alone and has hired himself out to Mr. Gibbs, who heads a hunting party in Cherokee Territory west of the Carolinas. For a year, Lafe works for the party as it moves from place to place on the trail of buffalo. In addition to the hardships of camp life, Lafe also suffers from loneliness and fear, and only one of the men is at all concerned about him. Lafe harbors the secret that his father has become a renegade—he has joined the Native Americans. Lafe is always afraid of the danger of the nearby Cherokees.

WILLIAM O. STEELE (1917–1979)
Winter Danger (1954; 180 PAGES; E/E)

Caje Amis's father is one of many men who have found it difficult to settle into a stable life on the frontier. He prefers to hunt, fish, and move from camp to camp. On the Tennessee frontier in the 1780's, Caje wishes to spend the coming hard winter in a cabin. His dream becomes reality when he and his father move in with relatives. However, Mr. Amis slips away, and Caje stays on to try to adjust to a settled life. He and the family struggle through a bad winter with less and less to eat. Caje learns what it is to live within a family, and what must be done to survive.

WILLIAM O. STEELE (1917–1979)
The Year of the Bloody Sevens (1963; 176 PAGES; E/E)

This story is about the movement westward that continued even during the Revolutionary War. After young Kelsey Bond's mother dies, Mr. Bond leaves their secure, settled home and goes to Logan's Fort in 1777 to help a friend. Meanwhile, Kelsey eagerly awaits word from his father in Kentucky. He receives a letter from his father, and sets out on the Wilderness Trail. From this point, the focus is on Kelsey's survival of a Native-American raid, his need to travel alone on the trail, his arrival at Logan's Fort, and his participation in a siege of the fort—which proves to Kelsey that he is courageous.

ROBERT J. STEELMAN (1914–   )
The Galvanized Reb (1977; 178 PAGES; E/E)

During the Civil War, a "galvanized reb" was a Confederate soldier converted to the cause of the Union. David Chantry is one such soldier—or so it seems. In order to free himself from prison, Chantry pretends to support the Northern cause. Because he knows how to use a camera, he is given an assignment by a Washington, D.C., newspaper to photograph the Oglala Sioux in the Idaho Territory. However, Chantry is secretly acting as a spy for the South; his real mission is to organize the Sioux to fight the nearby Union troops in their protected fort. Ultimately, Chantry's mission brings tragedy for him, the American Indians, and his cause.

JOHN STEINBECK (1902–1968)
The Grapes of Wrath (1939; ABOUT 616 PAGES; D/M)

A Nobel Prize–winning novel, *The Grapes of Wrath* is still a searing account of one family trying to survive during the Depression. The Joad family's odyssey begins in Oklahoma, where the land is drying up and the banks are repossessing farms. The Joads leave and drive to California. Along the way, they see hundreds of families moving west; soon they realize that there will be little work. Once in California, the Joads spend time in a government camp, then move on into grape harvesting and cotton picking. The novel builds to a climax in a driving storm, and reaches its still startling and frank conclusion in a railroad boxcar and barn. This is a social and historical document of an era that has become symbolic of dispossessed people everywhere.

DOROTHY STERLING
Mary Jane (1959; 201 PAGES; E/E)

Set shortly after the 1954 Supreme Court decision that ended segregation in the public schools, *Mary Jane* tells of the first year of integration in a southern school (Woodrow Wilson Junior High). Mary Jane and her friend Fred are the first African Americans to attend. They encounter the various types of hostility that blacks meet when coming into an all-white school. Mary Jane slowly adjusts. She eventually meets a white friend, Sally, who can see Mary Jane at school but not anywhere else. Their love of animals brings them together in a humorous incident with a squirrel. The new science club, which Sally and Mary Jane push to organize, adopts a rule that it will not visit places that do not allow blacks.

IRVING STONE (1903–1989)
Adversary in the House (1947; 432 PAGES; D/D)

Eugene V. Debs established the American Railway Union, helped organize labor strikes, and ran for President of the United States five times. In 1894, Debs was jailed for his part in a strike against Pullman Railway Cars; in 1918, he was imprisoned in a federal penitentiary for his opposition to World War I. This novel chronicles these and other historical events and personalities, focusing on Debs and his adversarial wife, Kate. As Debs's unionizing efforts expand to a nationwide focus, he begins to realize the inherent injustices in the class system promoted by capitalism. Socialism he finds equally alarming because of the violent tactics advocated by radicals. Settling on Democratic Socialism, Debs advocates nonviolent tactics and opposition to war with Germany. Throughout his career as a social reformer, Debs endures harsh criticism and personal injustices. His wife, Kate, is actually one of his main adversaries.

IRVING STONE (1903–1989)
Immortal Wife (1944; 450 PAGES; D/D)

From 1840 to 1890, John Charles Frémont was an explorer and topographer, the California Territory's first governor, a Free-Soil Democratic senator, the first Republican candidate for president, a general in the Union army, and governor of the Arizona Territory. This novel explores the theme that Frémont spends his lifetime seeking fame and fortune in compensation for his illegitimate birth. Jessie Benton is the intelligent, energetic, and highly ambitious daughter of famous Senator Thomas Hart Benton. While opposed to women's rights, Jessie believes a wife should be an active and equal partner in her husband's life. Married to Frémont in 1840, Jessie becomes his ghostwriter, editor, and advisor. Frémont's presidential candidacy is the first in which a wife is considered a factor in the candidate's fitness for office. Upon Frémont's death in 1890, Jessie continues to act as his agent, writing articles in praise of her husband and attacking in print those who dare to question his greatness.

IRVING STONE (1903–1989)
Love Is Eternal (1954; 462 PAGES; D/M)

Mary Todd Lincoln was one of the most misunderstood of American First Ladies. Inaccurate rumors of her mental instability and southern attitude toward slavery persisted long after her death. In the novel, Mary Todd is raised as a pampered southern belle. She catapults into a world of northern politics upon her marriage to reluctant bridegroom Abraham Lincoln of Springfield, Illinois. Mary is socially and politically ambitious for herself and her husband, and she shares his antislavery views. In 1865, she watches as her husband, the president, is shot to death in a Washington, D.C. theater. *Love Is Eternal* chronicles the Todd-Lincoln marriage, the differences the couple had in child-rearing attitudes, the death of one son and physical disabilities of another, and each spouse's strengths and weaknesses.

IRVING STONE (1903–1989)
The President's Lady (1951; 331 PAGES; M/M)

Married to a violent and unreasonable husband, Rachel Robards met frontier lawyer Andrew Jackson and fell in love. Unaware that her divorce had not been finalized, Rachel married Andrew, setting into motion a scandal which would haunt them forever. As Andrew fought to advance a political career, his enemies used the circumstances surrounding his marriage to Rachel to anger and defeat him. Set against this highly charged political backdrop, *The President's Lady* describes historical incidents from the presidency of George Washington through that of John Quincy Adams, recounting frontier skirmishes and the War of 1812. Rachel is a gentle and kind woman who must endure scandals while Andrew tries to acquire riches and political fame. When Jackson finally wins the presidency, his victory is tarnished by the sudden death of Rachel, who has been unable to withstand the onslaught of public shame and cruelty.

IRVING STONE (1903–1989)
Those Who Love (1965; 647 PAGES; D/D)

Abigail Smith, daughter of a Massachusetts Puritan minister and his wealthy wife, marries lawyer John Adams in the mid-eighteenth century. Their lives together take them from living under British rule through John's own service as president of the newly formed United States. Abigail and John write detailed letters to each other and provide information invaluable to the documentation of American history. Perhaps the most famous of the letters includes Abigail's request that the newly created government "remember the ladies." Although a Puritan wife, Abigail believes that an opportunity for true social, political, and religious freedom should include all Americans—not just white males. Her request is not taken seriously by John, who nonetheless concedes that his accomplishments would not have been possible without Abigail. Together, they create a family and help create a nation, providing it with two presidents.

HARRIET BEECHER STOWE (1811–1896)
Uncle Tom's Cabin (1852; ABOUT 560 PAGES; D/D)

Upon meeting Mrs. Stowe in the middle of the Civil War, President Lincoln supposedly said, "So, you are the little lady who has brought about this great war." Stowe's book has been one of the most widely read English-language works in the world; it was an instant best-seller on its publication in 1852. Stowe's novel chronicles the lives of several black families who suffer the bonds of slavery and seek escape into Ohio in the years before the Civil War. At the same time, white slave owners are presented sympathetically as people who manage a system, but who do not like the system they know to be evil. Interestingly, no other major literary figure of the period treated slavery in any extended work.

WILLIAM STYRON (1925–)
The Confessions of Nat Turner (1967; 425 PAGES; D/D)

The only known sustained revolt by black slaves took place in southeastern Virginia in 1831. The basis for this novel is a pamphlet dictated by the leader of the revolt, Nat Turner, to one of his jailers. The author tells Nat's tale in the form of a first-person narrative. He goes back in time to review his life as a slave and the lives of others around him. Nat also explains the background, the events, and the personalities that led to the ill-fated revolt. This is as much a psychological look into the essence of slavery as it is a history.

CHARLENE JOY TALBOT (1928–)
An Orphan for Nebraska (1979; ABOUT 208 PAGES; E/E)

The Children's Aid Society was formed in the middle of the nineteenth century to send homeless children to the West. This is the story of one of those children, orphan Kevin O'Rourke. Kevin's father has died in Ireland, and his mother has died aboard the ship to America. As a newsboy in New York in 1872, Kevin is miserable, poor, hungry, and bereft of the stability of a home. His one surviving relative, Uncle Michael, is in prison. Kevin discovers the Newsboys' Lodging House and is soon one of the children sent to the West. Finding a home and a job in a printing house, Kevin learns about the opportunities—and the harshness— of life in the largely unsettled country.

BOOTH TARKINGTON (1869–1946)
The Magnificent Ambersons (1918; 248 PAGES; M/M)

In the 1873–1916 era of American history, fabulous fortunes were made and spent on conspicuous consumption. A book of manners, Pulitzer Prize–winning *The Magnificent Ambersons* is also a historical chronicle of the decay and death of a period of idle, gracious living by families unaware that they have become outdated in their own lifetimes. The Ambersons are the social and economic leaders of their small town of Midland, Indiana. George Amberson Minafer, heir to the Amberson fortune, is convinced that persons of his class need not enter a profession or work. George fails to notice that his family's way of life is passing; a class of businesspeople and inventors is beginning to prevail. Midland becomes a sprawling industrial city, filled with working-class people. When George's mother dies, and there is no fortune left for George to inherit, he is forced to acknowledge that an era has passed.

MILDRED D. TAYLOR
Roll of Thunder, Hear My Cry (1976; 273 PAGES; M/M)

Deeply absorbing, this story follows the life of the Logans, an African-American family, for a year during the Depression in Mississippi. Cassie Logan, the main character, tells the story—which also involves her parents, her three brothers, an uncle, and a man who comes to work for her family. The Logans, the only blacks who own land in the area, make a determined attempt to keep the land in the face of falling prices for cotton and threats from the white mortgage holders. The year's events are framed by developments at Cassie's all-black school. Within this framework, Cassie suffers humiliation from a white girl, sees her parents try to fight the domination of white businesses, and fears the harm that may be done to her family by white men in the county.

MILDRED D. TAYLOR
Let the Circle Be Unbroken (1981; 394 PAGES; M/M)

Few full-length novels tracing the lives of African-American people from childhood to adulthood existed until recently. One such novel is this sequel to *Roll of Thunder, Hear My Cry*. *Let the Circle Be Unbroken* continues the narrative of the Logan family. The four Logan children are growing up in Mississippi in 1935, deep in the Depression years. Black experiences of rural sharecropping, interracial marriage, trial by all-white juries, and grinding poverty shared with white sharecroppers highlight the story. To survive the hardships, the Logan family abides by the virtues of hard work, pride, and self-respect.

MILDRED D. TAYLOR
The Friendship (1987; 53 PAGES; E/E)

This story of racial prejudice in the 1930's South is based on an incident in the life of the author's father. The black Logan children learn that pride and prejudice override friendship between a white store owner and an elderly black man. The store owner's name is John Wallace; while most blacks address most whites as "mister" or "missus," old Tom Bee addresses Wallace as "John." He does so because he once saved John's life, and because John has promised that Tom can address him by his first name. When Wallace is jeered by his white customers and his sons for allowing such familiarity, he orders Tom to call him "Mister Wallace." When Tom refuses, Wallace shoots him in the leg to appease his bigoted family and patrons. Dialogue is nonstandard English.

MILDRED D. TAYLOR
Mississippi Bridge (1990; 62 PAGES; E/E)

Another addition to the Logan family saga, this story highlights racial prejudice against African Americans in rural Mississippi in the 1930's. Jeremy Simms, a ten-year-old white boy, wants to be friends with the black Logan family. He finds it tough going, because his father and most of the townspeople are avid bigots who discourage friendships between the races. When blacks are forced off a bus to make room for late-arriving whites, bigotry inadvertently saves the lives of the blacks—when the bus goes off a bridge into the water below. Jeremy and Josia Logan work together to try to save lives as the bus quickly sinks, drowning the occupants. Both boys learn the value of working toward a common goal. Nonstandard English is used in both the narrative and dialogue.

CRYSTAL THRASHER (1921–)
The Dark Didn't Catch Me (1975; 179 PAGES; M/M)

During the Great Depression—a period of hardships on a scale unique in American history—Seely Robinson's father sells their family farm without telling even her mother. He moves the family into the southern Indiana hills so he can get work cutting timber. In the Depression, there is no choice; the family moves to find work—only to find an equally tough life. Seely's father is away during the week, and bitterness grows between him and her mother. A neighbor commits suicide when he can no longer find work. Seely has a difficult time adjusting to school and new friends. When the family is finally able to leave the area, though, Seely knows she will miss the hills.

CRYSTAL THRASHER (1921–   )
Between Dark and Daylight (1979; 248 PAGES; M/M)

In this continuation of *The Dark Didn't Catch Me,* the attention is on relationships among three families in rural southern Indiana during the Depression. Seely Robinson's family is moving again, now that her father has found a job in another county. Their old truck breaks down on the way, and the family is forced to stay at an empty house in the woods. Seely's family becomes acquainted with the Meader family, and Seely becomes fast friends with Johnny Meader and his friend Byron. Lurking in the background are the Fender twins, strange sons of Nellie Fender; Nellie has actually warned Seely about her boys. A violent incident at the end of the novel affects Seely's life from then on.

CRYSTAL THRASHER (1921–   )
End of a Dark Road (1982; 214 PAGES; M/M)

The third novel in the series about the Robinson family, *End of a Dark Road* finds Seely Robinson now in high school in Oolitic, Indiana—a long bus ride from her home in the southern hills. Winter has come, her father is out of work, and the family is on welfare. Seely sees how the Depression affects not only her family but those around her. Her friend Annabel, also facing hardships, used to be from a well-to-do family. Her friend Russell becomes more withdrawn as his stepfather increasingly abuses him. Seely's father dies an early death, and her mother must work even harder. Despite these problems, Seely is a strong young woman from a caring family. At the close of the novel, Mrs. Robinson decides to move out of the harsh hills to make a new start.

CRYSTAL THRASHER (1921–   )
A Taste of Daylight (1984; 204 PAGES; E/E)

This is the fourth novel in the series about the Robinson family. In Depression-era Indiana, seventeen-year-old Seely and her family live in the hills of Greene County. When her father dies, however, her mother moves Seely and her younger brother to the city of Bedford. Life in the city is a shock to them all. They had not known that money was the overriding concern of city people. Water is not free for the taking, as it was in the hills, and it seems that city people pay for services which are considered neighborly favors in the hills. Worse, the Depression-ridden economy of 1937 makes jobs scarce, and a person has to work for low wages. The "taste of daylight" that Seely's mother escapes from the hills to acquire proves a costly learning experience for the family.

ANN TURNER (1945–)
Grasshopper Summer (1989; 166 PAGES; E/E)

Following the Civil War, young Sam White and his family leave their Kentucky homeland for a fresh start in the Dakotas. Sam loves Kentucky and living with his grandparents. But for Sam's father, Kentucky is a daily, sad reminder of the recent bloody Civil War. Their journey west is hard, as is living in a sod house while trying to farm their newly acquired land. Just when things are going well, grasshoppers descend, eating all of the crops. Surviving this challenge, the White family resolves to meet all future crises with the fortitude and togetherness they have achieved.

MARK TWAIN (1835–1910)
Adventures of Huckleberry Finn (1884; 245 PAGES; M/D)

This novel, by one of the country's most famous authors, is set in Missouri in the 1840's. Huck Finn is the son of the town drunkard, who beats him. To escape the brutality and the efforts of his aunt to civilize him, Huck runs away. He meets Jim, a runaway slave, and they begin an eleven-hundred-mile journey down the Mississippi River on a raft, theoretically to help Jim find freedom. In the last major portion of the plot, the quest for Jim's freedom from slavery shifts to Jim's and Huck's search for freedom from all the constraints of society. This is reflected in Huck's last remark: "I reckon I got to light out for the territory ahead of the rest, because Aunt Sally she's going to adopt me and civilize me, and I can't stand it." A multilayered novel, Twain's work also marked advances in American literary style. The novel reflects period attitudes toward blacks, and racist language is used.

MARK TWAIN (1835–1910)
Tom Sawyer (1876; ABOUT 312 PAGES; M/D)

Tom Sawyer may be read as a period piece about a small town in the mid-1800's, an exploration into how children behave among themselves and how they view adults, and an examination of the restraints of adult society as Twain perceived them in the pre-Civil-War era. Tom is a boy growing up in St. Petersburg, Missouri, on the Mississippi River, probably in the 1840's or 1850's. His famous adventures include a fence whitewashing, a pirate adventure on Jackson's Island, the witness of a murder in a graveyard, interaction with evil Injun Joe, the discovery of a real treasure, and entrapment in a cave. In these escapades, Tom is joined by Huckleberry Finn, Becky Thatcher, Judge Thatcher, Aunt Polly, and other unforgettable American literary characters. *Tom Sawyer* reflects racist attitudes and language of the period when it was written.

YOSHIKO UCHIDA (1921–1992)

Samurai of Gold Hill (1972; 113 PAGES; E/E)

Samurai of Gold Hill is about Japanese immigrants, who were among the many groups of pioneers in America. In 1869, when the Japanese feudal system crumbles in battle and the emperor is restored to power, a defeated group leaves for California. They take with them seedlings and silkworms to set up a tea and silk farm at Gold Hill. Once at their Gold Hill colony, they face many obstacles and are objects of curiosity and prejudice. Since the immigrants come from an orderly, feudal, warrior society, they are unsuited to the rude, boisterous post-Gold-Rush era. They eventually also find that the soil and weather are not suitable for their type of farming. This colony, named Wakamatsu after their original home in Japan, did exist and eventually fail. A glossary of Japanese terms is included.

YOSHIKO UCHIDA (1921–1992)

A Jar of Dreams (1981; 128 PAGES; E/E)

Only in recent years has there been much full-scale investigation into Japanese-American lives in the United States between the wars and during World War II. This story focuses on eleven-year-old Rinko, who lives with her family in California during the Depression. Rinko wants to be like everyone else, but because she is Japanese, she looks different. Her father runs a barbershop, which suffers a decline in business. Her mother begins to take in laundry to pay bills. During the summer that the novel takes place, Rinko's aunt Waka arrives from Japan. She provides added strength when violence threatens the family and tragedy comes to Rinko's younger brother.

YOSHIKO UCHIDA (1921–1992)

Journey to Topaz (1971; 149 PAGES; E/E)

In 1942, thousands of Japanese—most of whom were American citizens—were held in concentration camps and considered enemy aliens because of America's war with Japan. As *Journey to Topaz* begins, eleven-year-old Yuki Sakane and her family are living a happy and prosperous life in Berkeley, California. When President Franklin Roosevelt issues an order forcing the removal of Japanese from the West Coast, Yuki's father is arrested and detained by the FBI. Yuki, her mother, and brother Ken are sent to a concentration camp in the barren desert of Utah. Although they have committed no crimes and are loyal to America, the Sakanes and thousands of other Japanese are treated as prisoners of war. After nearly a year passes in the camp, Yuki's family is reunited with her father and released from the camp to live in Salt Lake City. In order to prove the family's loyalty to America, Ken enlists in the United States Army as a part of a special Japanese unit.

YOSHIKO UCHIDA (1921–1992)
Journey Home (1978; 131 PAGES; E/E)

A companion to *Journey to Topaz,* this is the story of the Sakane family after their release from a concentration camp for Japanese and Japanese Americans in the Utah desert. Twelve-year-old Yuki and her parents live in a cramped apartment in Salt Lake City. They yearn to return home to California and their former, comfortable way of life. Yuki's father, once a prosperous businessman, is now a low-paid shipping clerk; her mother is forced to work as a domestic. Brother Ken is recuperating from leg wounds suffered fighting for the United States in the war against Japan. Although happy to be out of the concentration camp, the Sakanes still face prejudice daily from Americans distrustful of Asians. Yuki's father is still under surveillance by the FBI. Finally, the ban preventing Japanese Americans from living on the West Coast is lifted, and the Sakanes are happy to return to their beloved California.

BETTY UNDERWOOD (1921–)
The Tamarack Tree (1971; 230 PAGES; M/M)

Bernadette Savard comes to Canterbury, Connecticut, in 1833. She is going to help Hester and David Fry and their family and also go to school at the female seminary. Bernadette is an African-American orphan who has been taken in by Fry's brother and his family who live in Ohio. She hopes to be educated at Canterbury, then go to Oberlin College in Ohio, the first college to admit women and minority students. However, when she arrives at Canterbury, she finds that Prudence Crandall (the teacher) is not admitting "girls of color" to the school, which dashes Bernadette's hopes. As she grapples with the problems of slavery and education for women, Bernadette is also forced to face the future—which appears to be a shrinking world for women.

DALE VAN EVERY (1896–1976)
The Day the Sun Died (1971; 315 PAGES; M/M)

In 1890, a Paiute Indian prophet has a vision that the Messiah will return with dead Native Americans returned to life, the land will again belong to Native Americans, and whites will retreat across the ocean. Word spreads among the whites about increasing occurrences of the Ghost Dance, during which Indians call for the return of their Messiah and the reclaiming of their land. Violence toward the Indians escalates—and culminates in the Battle of Wounded Knee in South Dakota. The cast of characters in this novel includes a self-serving army lieutenant, a Dartmouth-educated Sioux Indian, a hardened mountain man, a half-breed courageous young woman, and the famous western artist Remington. Women are portrayed as coy teases, sexual prey, or beasts of burden.

GORE VIDAL (1925–)
Burr (1973; 425 PAGES; D/D)

Aaron Burr (1756–1836) was one of the most puzzling figures in early American history. He served in the American Revolution and became a hero. He was Jefferson's vice-president. But, he killed Alexander Hamilton in a duel, and Jefferson accused him of plotting to make the western territories into an empire controlled by Burr. In the novel *Burr,* Vidal's technique is to work all of these facts into the form of a memoir—told partly by Burr and partly by a young journalist, a fictional character. This technique allows all of the actual persons with whom Burr comes into contact—such as Washington, Jefferson, Hamilton, Jackson, and Madison—to enter the story. The technique also allows a vivid recreation of the events in which Burr participated.

GORE VIDAL (1925–)
1876 (1976; 369 PAGES; D/D)

America's centennial year marked its most controversial presidential election—the contest between Rutherford B. Hayes and Samuel Tilden. The election was decided in the House of Representatives. Into this lowest point of United States history comes fictional Charles Schuyler. His finances depleted in the Panic of 1873, Charlie returns to the U.S. from Europe with his daughter Emma, a widowed princess. Charlie hopes to write about the centennial, become good friends with favored candidate Tilden, marry Emma to a suitable American, and return to Europe as a diplomat. Instead, he becomes involved in the intrigues of the election and is drawn into the social and political power struggles of a nation about to become an empire.

GORE VIDAL (1925–)
Empire (1987; 486 PAGES; D/D)

Caroline Sanford, French-educated heiress and illegitimate descendant of Aaron Burr, becomes a publisher of power in Washington, D.C., in the 1890's. She is in competition with publisher William Randolph Hearst, who made news rather than just report it. America is changing drastically at the turn of the century, and moneymen are looking for new areas of economic opportunity. Thus, expansion is necessary. But to expand beyond the United States borders, a war is needed. Hearst leads the country to war with a headline concerning Spanish intentions; before long, Guam, Puerto Rico, and the Philippines are U.S. possessions in 1898 as a result of the Spanish-American War.

GORE VIDAL (1925–   )
Washington, D.C. (1967; 377 PAGES; M/M)

In the years 1937 to 1952, Washington, D.C., is a clubby town. It is run by powerful politicians and newspaper publishers, who often wield political life and death by the slant of their coverage. Major political battles form over President Franklin Roosevelt's New Deal policies and possible involvement of the U.S. in World War II. Politicians run scared as McCarthyism gains force. During this period, James Burden Day is a powerful senator of long tenure and minimal corruption. His young assistant is amoral and eagerly corrupt. Both men dream of being president. Senator Day's career is shattered when his former assistant, now a congressman, threatens to expose one incident of corruption in Day's otherwise honest political history. The congressman then goes on to campaign for Day's senate seat—and, eventually, the presidency.

ALICE WALKER (1944–   )
The Color Purple (1982; 295 PAGES; D/D)

The Color Purple chronicles southern life for black women from the 1920's to the 1950's. Celie is a homely and lonely young woman. Sexually abused by her stepfather, Celie leads a life of neglect and low self-esteem. After marrying a moderately successful farmer, Celie is physically and verbally abused by him until his former lover, Shug Avery, comes to recuperate from an illness. A traveling blues singer, Shug Avery helps Celie confront her abusive husband and gain the confidence to finally leave him. Meanwhile, Celie's sister-in-law is beaten brutally and jailed for "sassing" the mayor's wife in a nearby village. Upon her release, she has no will to live until she witnesses the downtrodden Celie's confrontation with her husband. Alice Walker won a Pulitzer Prize for this novel. The novel contains extensive use of black dialect and sexual situations.

ALICE WALKER (1944–   )
Meridian (1976; 220 PAGES; M/M)

Meridian chronicles racism, sexism, and interracial relationships. Meridian is a black girl raised in the deep South in the 1960's by her gentle, dreamy father—a schoolteacher and farmer—and her pious, bitter mother—a former schoolteacher. At seventeen, Meridian becomes pregnant and marries. Like her mother, Meridian sees marriage and children as a burden. Unlike her mother, however, Meridian gives away her child in order to attend college. Once there, she is unable to accept black revolutionary ideas about the use of violence to obtain freedom. Believing that African Americans can attain power through voting, Meridian embarks on a journey throughout the rural South. She has a personal and political impact as she struggles to register blacks to vote. The novel contains obscene language and sexual situations.

MARGARET WALKER (1915–)
Jubilee (1965; ABOUT 413 PAGES; D/D)

This is a depiction of African-American family life before, during, and after the Civil War in Georgia and Alabama. The author follows a young slave girl, Vyry, who is the daughter of the white plantation owner, from childhood into middle-adult years. Vyry marries a free black man and bears him two children, but he disappears in the war. Meanwhile, the plantation where she lives is ruined in the war and is sold in the postwar years. Hearing nothing from her husband, Vyry leaves with another man and marries him. During this marriage, the two suffer from the problems of racial violence and attempt to build a life on various farms. The first husband reappears at the end of the novel, and Vyry is forced to make a decision about her future. *Jubilee* contains dialect and adult language.

WILLARD M. WALLACE (1911–)
Jonathan Dearborn (1967; 369 PAGES; M/M)

Jonathan Dearborn is the son of a minister in Portland, Maine. He has just graduated from college and is about to begin practice as a lawyer when the war with Britain begins in 1812. Since he has spent two years at sea, Jonathan decides to sign on the brig *Argus* as a privateersman. Jonathan's adventures provide the background for an account of the War of 1812 in all of its aspects until the peace treaty is signed on Christmas Eve, 1814. There are descriptions of life at sea, a Maine farm, an English prison, and drawing-room scenes of Europe. The novel also includes presentations of the Federalist Party's point of view, the Republican Party's philosophy, and the international interests in the war.

LUKE WALLIN (1943–)
In the Shadow of the Wind (1984; 203 PAGES; E/E)

In the winter of 1835, Creek Indians in their ancestral lands of Alabama fight to survive white invasion. The once fruitful forests are barren and silent, and the lifestyle of the Native Americans is changing. Into the Creek lands comes Caleb McElroy, a sixteen-year-old white boy. Living with his mother on an Alabama plantation, Caleb befriends Pine Basket, a sixteen-year-old Creek Indian girl. Hired white men kill Native Americans wantonly, and herd others en masse to a land farther west. Caleb intercepts this exodus, rescuing and later marrying Pine Basket.

ROBERT PENN WARREN (1905–1989)
All the King's Men (1946; ABOUT 461 PAGES; D/D)

Willie Stark is a well-known literary character; he is also a superbly drawn American politician of the 1930's. Robert Penn Warren paints a searing, complex word portrait of Stark through the eyes of one of his aides, Jack Burden. Burden chronicles the rise of Stark from 1922 until he becomes governor of a mythical southern state in 1933. The focus of the story then shifts to the period from 1936 to 1939, during which Burden uncovers the secrets of Stark's political foes and watches Stark as he considers running for a Senate seat. As Burden investigates, he peels away layers of a corrupt society and uncovers old mysteries. Stark is assassinated at the end of the novel. This portrait is supposedly based on 1930's Louisiana politician Huey Long. The author uses adult situations and frank language.

MANLY WADE WELLMAN (1903–1986)
Battle for King's Mountain (1962; 170 PAGES; E/E)

The 1780 Battle of King's Mountain, South Carolina, proved to be a significant turning point in favor of the American side against Great Britain in the Revolutionary War. Zack Harper, from North Carolina, appears in this second of a series of novels that deals with his role as a scout in Major Chronicle's company of scouts in the Continental Army. Zack and the company follow the British Tories under their resourceful commander, Colonel Patrick Ferguson, until his army is entrenched on King's Mountain. The novel details the preparations and the battle, and indicates the honor and loyalty on both sides.

MANLY WADE WELLMAN (1903–1986)
Jamestown Adventure (1967; 192 PAGES; E/E)

Wellman places a fictional character—young James Rickard—into the story of the first years of the Jamestown, Virginia, colony in 1608–1609. Jamie, the cousin of Captain John Smith, is sent by Smith to live among the Algonquin Indians. He becomes acquainted with Chief Powhatan, his daughter Pocahontas, and a half-brother Opechancanough, who wants to be the next chief. Jamie must be cautious. His skill with a bow and as a wrestler causes jealousy among the Indian braves, while his relationship with John Smith causes some suspicion among the white settlers. Jamie helps the struggling colony and tries to prevent a rebellion by Powhatan's people against him.

MANLY WADE WELLMAN (1903–1986)
The South Fork Rangers (1963; 171 PAGES; E/E)

Southerners fought for the United States long before they sought to separate from it. In this novel, Zack Harper and a group of North Carolina friends, the South Fork Rangers, prepare to play their part in the South's actions in the Revolutionary War. Their task is to capture a Tory officer named Robinson Alspaye, who is known to be a dangerous and vengeful ally of the British. Alspaye is also shrewd and competent, and he eludes the Rangers as they track him. Zack and his friends hear news of the continuing battles elsewhere. Finally, Alspaye is cornered in a cave and killed. Zack participates in the surrender of British General Cornwallis at Yorktown.

JESSAMYN WEST (1902–1984)
The Massacre at Fall Creek (1975; 308 PAGES; M/M)

A little-known (although many-times repeated) event occurred at Fall Creek, Indiana, in 1824: Five white men killed nine American Indians. Violence between whites and Indians was certainly common in this period—and long after. However, the event produced a unique result. For the first time recorded, the white men were tried, convicted, and three were hanged. West creates her story from these elements. The narrative covers the killings, the trial, and the aftermath of the murders. One man escapes. Because of his youth, one man is saved by a reprieve from the governor. Three main characters view the events: Charlie Fort, a defense lawyer; Hannah Cape, Fort's friend; and Handsome Lake, a Native-American prophet.

JESSAMYN WEST (1902–1984)
Except for Me and Thee (1949; 306 PAGES; M/M)

A companion to *The Friendly Persuasion*, this novel expands and develops the lives of Jess and Eliza Birdwell, who are Irish Quakers. They meet when Eliza is beginning her career as a minister and marry shortly after. For the first five years and three children of their married life, they live with Jess's parents in Ohio, then move to Indiana to build their own home. These are troubled times for America in the 1840's and 1850's, and the Birdwells become involved in the slavery controversy. Trying to remain true to their religion, they remain out of the Civil War. However, some of their children want to experiment with other ways, and daughter Mattie marries a soldier who is a Methodist. When Jess comments on how worldly people have become, Eliza answers, "Except for me and thee."

JESSAMYN WEST (1902–1984)
The Friendly Persuasion (1945; 211 PAGES; M/M)

Using several loosely related incidents, *The Friendly Persuasion* examines Quaker attitudes toward war, neighbors, religion, the law, family life, and occupation. Jess and Eliza Birdwell are Irish Quakers who live in southern Indiana in the pre-Civil-War and Civil-War era. The reader meets them late in life, after decades of marriage and several children. Jess works at a garden nursery and Eliza follows her calling as a Quaker minister. A quiet story, *The Friendly Persuasion* examines its characters within the context of their Quaker heritage and daily life.

MORRIS L. WEST (1916–   )
The Ambassador (1965; 272 PAGES; M/M)

Arising out of the early Vietnam War era, this novel explores the dilemmas of United States policy toward South Vietnam. Ambassador Maxwell Amberley is asked to leave his post as ambassador to Japan to take on the task of being ambassador to South Vietnam. As Amberley states his problems, ". . . all I had to do, to rally the country and win the war, was to have the Generals chop off his head." Amberley's reference is to Phung Van Cung, president-dictator of the country. Much like a fairy tale, a story develops as relationships are examined between the shaky Vietnamese government and the U.S. military, the Vietnamese government and local U.S. officials, and Amberley and those around him.

EDITH WHARTON (1862–1937)
The House of Mirth (1905; ABOUT 317 PAGES; D/D)

The House of Mirth is about wealthy and shallow society people at the turn of the nineteenth and twentieth centuries in New York. Lily Bart believes that she is a part of a meaningful lifestyle. One of few unmarried women on the social scene, beautiful and gracious, Lily is sought after as a guest. However, Lily is unaware that she is perceived merely as a desirable decoration for fashionable gatherings. She searches in vain for a soul mate who has status and money. Eventually cast out from the society that has used and objectified her, Lily is forced to live in reduced circumstances, financially and emotionally adrift. A social history, book of manners, and commentary on the status of unattached women, *The House of Mirth* exposes the follies of wealth devoid of humanity or principles.

ROBB WHITE (1909–)
Flight Deck (1961; 210 PAGES; E/E)

About half of this novel is concerned with flight deck operations aboard the aircraft carrier *Enterprise* during World War II. In this part of the story, young navy pilot John Lawrence is just out of aviation school. During the Pacific Battle of Midway in August 1942, John is wounded severely enough to be permanently grounded. Assigned to a desk job as an operations officer on the *Enterprise,* John is determined to find a more useful job. In the second half of the book, he slips away to a deserted island with the help of his pilot brother, Jeff, and becomes a spotter for the Marines. Remaining unidentified in his radio calls, John performs a valuable service and saves a young boy.

ROBB WHITE (1909–)
Surrender (1966; 230 PAGES; M/M)

The Japanese attacked the Philippine Islands at almost the same time as they attacked Pearl Harbor in December 1941. This story concentrates on the five months after the attack on the U.S. Naval Base at Cavite in the Philippines. The main characters are young Juan and Juanita MacGregor, who become involved in all parts of the defense of the islands. Along with them are chief motor machinist's mate Dave Gannon, who befriends the youngsters and later is saved by them, and radar expert George Fowler, who is both overbearing and helpless, but redeems himself. The story climaxes with the march of 78,000 soldiers along the Bataan Peninsula and the surrender of 12,000 defenders of the fortress on Corregidor.

ROBB WHITE (1909–)
Torpedo Run (1962; 183 PAGES; E/E)

During World War II, the PT boat—at about 80 feet long with a crew of 12—was the smallest warship in the Navy. Moving at 60 miles per hour, PT boats were designed to hit and run quickly. Captain Jones and Executive Officer Peter Brent command the PT boat dubbed *Slewfoot* by its combat-hardened crew. Near New Guinea, in the South Pacific, the men hide by day and operate at night. When Captain Jones is killed, a new captain—Adrian Archer—arrives, fresh from officers' school. What develops is the classic moral and military story of a crew pitted against a man who is perceived as a poor commander. Peter Brent plays a leading role in the dilemma about authority as the *Slewfoot* engages in one dangerous mission after another.

ROBB WHITE (1909–)
Up Periscope (1956; 240 PAGES; M/M)

In 1943, the war in the Pacific still raged despite a major United States naval victory at Midway. Ken Braden, whose father and brother are in Japanese prison camps, volunteers for a mission aboard the submarine *Shark*. Fresh from underwater demolition school, he still does not swim well and has never been in a submarine. The *Shark* crew is suffering from morale problems after a lengthy shift at sea, and the captain does not enjoy the men's confidence. Under these conditions, the *Shark* glides to its destination—a Japanese-held island from which Ken must steal a code. Life on a sub, the death of the captain in a courageous act, brushes with the enemy, and details of Ken's mission make up the plot.

LEONARD WIBBERLEY (1915–1983)
John Treegate's Musket (1959; 181 PAGES; M/M)

The first of a series of novels about the Treegates, *John Treegate's Musket* covers the years 1769 to 1775 in Boston. John Treegate has fought against the French in the Battle of Quebec and considers himself a loyal British subject. He thinks that complaints about King George III, taxation, and interference with local government are at best, exaggerated, and at worst, treasonous. He teaches his son, Peter, to be loyal also. However, over the next six years, John begins to change his mind about the colonists' position. Finally, in 1775, he takes his musket and gives one to Peter, and they set out for the Battle of Bunker Hill to fight the British.

LEONARD WIBBERLEY (1915–1983)
Peter Treegate's War (1960; 153 PAGES; E/E)

The second of a series, this volume begins with the Battle of Bunker Hill in Massachusetts in 1775 and Peter Treegate's role in the battle. His father, John Treegate, is also in the Revolutionary army. Peter's adventures carry him through the end of 1776—a period when the army is ill-equipped, badly trained, and seldom paid. Before the Battle of Trenton, New Jersey, Washington must address the troops to convince them to reenlist. One of Peter's other concerns is his "foster" father, a Scotsman named the MacLaren of Spey, who would like to reinstate the Scottish clan system in the colonies—a futile cause which brings his death. A new character, Peace of God Manly, a sea captain who helps the colonists, is introduced.

LEONARD WIBBERLEY (1915–1983)
Sea Captain from Salem (1961; 181 PAGES; E/E)

In the third volume of this series, Peace of God Manly, the sea captain from Salem, sails his war sloop to France, where he receives sealed orders from Benjamin Franklin. Franklin is trying to convince the French to aid the colonists during the critical period from 1777 to 1778, when the British blockade endangers the colonial effort. Peace of God Manly mixes with the aging Franklin, the French foreign minister, the British First Lord of the Admiralty, and the British Earl of Chatham, who before the war has spoken on behalf of the colonists.

LEONARD WIBBERLEY (1915–1983)
Treegate's Raiders (1962; 215 PAGES; E/E)

The concluding book about the Revolutionary War in the Treegate series opens in 1780, with the war at a stalemate. Peter Treegate, who first saw battle at Bunker Hill, is now in the South, where he is convinced the war will come to a climax. Peter heads a band of Carolina mountaineers, who can fight in the mountains. Treegate's raiders see action at King's Mountain and Cowpens, two of the smaller but significant battles. Peter is also present at Yorktown, Virginia, where the British and their German allies surrender. The British band deliberately play "The World Turned Upside Down" out of tune.

LEONARD WIBBERLEY (1915–1983)
Leopard's Prey (1971; 181 PAGES; E/E)

This is a continuation of the Treegate saga. It is 1807, and Peter Treegate is now fifty years old and a prosperous merchant in Salem, Massachusetts. He has long been married to Peace of God Manly's daughter, Nancy. Into the household comes Manly Treegate, orphaned nephew of Peter's brother. Chafing under his uncle's discipline and eager to go to sea, Manly convinces his uncle to allow him to go on a business trip to Norfolk, Virginia. There, in the bay, a British ship fires on an American ship and impresses three seamen. Manly is captured by the same ship, the *Leopard*. He begins a lengthy service on the ship in the Caribbean. Eventually, he returns to his family in Salem.

LEONARD WIBBERLEY (1915–1983)
Red Pawns (1973; 180 PAGES; M/M)

Continuing the Treegate saga, the author relates the events surrounding the buildup to the War of 1812 between the young United States and Great Britain. Manly Treegate, a sailor of eighteen, goes to the frontier area of the Northwest Territory. His uncle, shipowner Peter Treegate, sails to London to try to work out economic problems between the two countries. Manly and his brother Peter join General William Henry Harrison's militia and battle the great Indian Chief Tecumseh and his followers. The scene shifts between events on the frontier and events in London. At the end of the novel, the War of 1812 begins.

LEONARD WIBBERLEY (1915–1983)
The Last Battle (1976; 194 PAGES; M/M)

The Treegate family saga concludes with a focus on the course of the War of 1812 between the United States and Great Britain. Manly Treegate is the captain of the ship *Wild Duck* in the young U.S. Navy. On the ship is his younger brother, Peter, who wants to be in the service but chafes under the discipline of his older brother. In Europe, their uncle, Major Peter Treegate, wants to obtain French aid for the United States. Finally, the three Treegates meet in the Battle of New Orleans at Christmas, 1814, when Andrew Jackson leads the U.S. against the British.

TOM WICKER (1926–)
Unto This Hour (1984; 633 PAGES; D/D)

Exhaustive research and considerable time produced this novel about the August 28–30, 1862, Civil War Battle of Second Manassas—or Second Bull Run, as the South and North respectively named the conflict. Several famous wartime figures enter the conflict: Stonewall Jackson, Robert E. Lee, James Longstreet, J.E.B. Stuart, John Pope, and George McClellan. In addition, Wicker introduces many fictional persons from both sides who intersect with the actual persons. In a poorly mapped area of northern Virginia, a complex campaign is carried out to a significant conclusion for the entire war.

JOHN A. WILLIAMS (1925–)
Captain Blackman (1972; 323 PAGES; M/M)

An unusual novel with a definite point of view, this is the story of a black soldier in the midst of the Vietnam War. The soldier, Captain Abraham Blackman, is pinned down by enemy fire and then wounded. As he suffers from the wound and waits for his rescuers, he begins to go in and out of consciousness and dream of the role of the African-American soldier in American wars. He imagines himself fighting in scenes from all of the major encounters: the Revolution, the Battle of New Orleans in the War of 1812, the Civil War, the Indian Wars, the Spanish-American War, and World Wars I and II. He is proud of the role his people have played, but bitter about the lack of progress toward true freedom and equality. Frank language is used.

OWEN WISTER (1860–1938)
The Virginian (1902; ABOUT 434 PAGES; D/D)

Even in 1902, there was a wistfulness about the passing of the American frontier and the special people it created. When Wister's novel first appeared, the frontier had been officially "closed" only since 1890, but his reflective series of episodes is clearly nostalgic. Wister created a type: the tall, easygoing, slow-talking, fast-drawing hero, who became the tall, silent, handsome man of so many Western stories to come. The Virginian is a transplanted ranch hand who has lived in Wyoming from 1874 to 1890. He is one of the last of the horsemen to deal with cattle, harsh weather, cattle rustling, outlaws, and the pretty young schoolteacher from the East, whom he marries in the end.

RICHARD WORMSER (1908–)
The Black Mustanger (1971; 183 PAGES; E/E)

The Rikers live in Tennessee during the post-Civil-War period, when all sections of the country are rebuilding—especially the South. Mr. Riker (who served in the Union Army) and his family hope to forget their war-torn state and move to Texas. There, Mr. Riker gets a job branding wild cattle and building a new herd. He progresses until he breaks his leg. Having served in the Union Army makes Mr. Riker isolated in Texas, as he had also felt in Tennessee. Thirteen-year-old son Dan is desperate for help until a half-black, half-Apache mustanger, Will Mesteno, agrees to give Dan a job. How Dan becomes Will's partner—in a period when working with an African American was unknown—forms the theme of the remainder of the story.

HERMAN WOUK (1915–   )
The Winds of War (1971; 882 PAGES; D/D)

Using the literary device of placing the same character in all of the important places in a story, Wouk spins a lengthy, complex saga of U.S. Navy officer Victor Henry and his family from 1939 to 1941 and the attack on Pearl Harbor. Because "Pug" Henry's job as naval attaché takes him to many geographic locations, he sees the beginnings and the evolution of the war in Europe, the horror of Hitler's Nazi German regime, the situation in Italy, and the resistance of the British. In addition to Henry, other main characters are Natalie Jastrow, an American Jewish girl living in Italy; Alistair Tudsbury, a British war correspondent; Pamela Tudsbury, his daughter, who is in the British military; and Henry's wife, sons, and daughter. Famous people such as Hitler, Churchill, Roosevelt, and Stalin also march across the scene.

HERMAN WOUK (1915–   )
War and Remembrance (1978; 555 PAGES; D/D)

The next installment of Wouk's World War II saga covers the period from the attack on Pearl Harbor in December 1941 to the end of 1942. During this period, the United States fought significant naval battles in the Pacific at Midway and Guadalcanal, and the British achieved a breakthrough in Africa at El Alamein. Wouk moves his characters through these events by placing U.S. Navy officer Victor Henry in the sea battles, his son Bryan in submarine warfare, and his son Warren in aerial combat. Famous naval commanders such as Halsey, Spruance, Nimitz, and Kimmel also enter the scene. The plight of Natalie Jastrow, an American Jew in Europe, continues, as do the activities of British war correspondent Alistair Tudsbury and his daughter Pamela.

RICHARD WRIGHT (1908–1960)
Native Son (1940; 392 PAGES; D/D)

In the 1940's, life in Chicago too often held little for the city's African-American population. Wright incorporates the lives of several African Americans into the character of Bigger Thomas, who lives with his mother and siblings in a one-room shack. Most of Bigger's emotions are rooted in hatred, fear and frustration resulting from the white control over his world. On the other side of town in a wealthy white neighborhood lives Mr. Dalton, a slum landlord who has bought his family a "social conscience" by donating money to black organizations. Bigger is hired as Dalton's chauffeur. Shortly thereafter he murders Dalton's daughter. The murder releases in Bigger a feeling of freedom and control he has never before experienced. An expert and compassionate white lawyer tries to have Bigger's sentence mitigated by explaining the rage and suffering experienced by young black men. Bigger is sentenced to death.

LAURENCE YEP (1948–)
The Star Fisher (1991; 147 PAGES; E/E)

In 1927, fifteen-year-old Joan Lee is an American citizen born of Chinese immigrant parents. Moving from Ohio to Clarksburg, West Virginia, the Lees are in search of a new start for their laundry business and a place to call home. In Clarksburg, they experience prejudice and are ostracized by many of the townspeople. When their landlady befriends them, the Lees begin to feel more comfortable. Finally, the hard work and integrity displayed by the Lees wins them approval. Their most tenacious harassers are faced down by their elderly, widely respected landlady. A secondary theme involves Joan's friendship with a kind and dignified young girl who has also been alienated from the town because of her family's involvement in the theater—an occupation deemed socially unacceptable by the narrow-minded citizens of Clarksburg.

JANE YOLEN
The Gift of Sarah Barker (1981; 155 PAGES; E/E)

The rigorous life of Shakers provides the basis for this novel. Sarah and her mother travel to New Vale, New York, in the mid-1800's to become Shakers. Since there can be only one mother and one father among Shakers, Sarah's mother is henceforth known only as "sister" to Sarah and all other Believers. Although she tries to be a good Shaker, Sarah dreams of her long-ago worldly life, when she has a father, and her mother is her mother. A fellow Shaker, Brother Abel, who is an orphan, also dreams of a more worldly life. Abel and Sarah both lead the tormented life of those who need physical as well as spiritual contact with other human beings. After Sarah's mother commits suicide, Abel openly consoles Sarah; both are banished from the village. Sarah finds her father, and she and Abel find happiness outside the Shaker village together.

BLAINE M. YORGASON
Massacre at Salt Creek (1979; 183 PAGES; M/M)

Utah Territory in 1858 is in the middle of a war against Native Americans when this story begins. Five Mormons—a married couple, two men, and an infant—are traveling unarmed. They are attacked by a party of Ute Indians. The only survivors are the wife, the infant, and a half-crazed Ute Indian named Inepegut (which means "crazy" in Ute language). The woman escapes with the baby and begins a long, torturous fight for survival. They are pursued by the Utes, and the story reaches an unexpected ending. A memorial plaque stands today in Salt Creek Canyon on the spot where the actual massacre took place.

ALIDA E. YOUNG
Land of the Iron Dragon (1978; 200 PAGES; E/E)

Ten thousand Chinese laborers built American railroads in the late 1800's; however, none were mentioned when the work was completed. This is a story about two of those people. Driven out of their homeland of China by hardship and rebellion, young Lim Yan-sung and his father come to San Francisco in 1862. They hope to build a new life and send money to Lim's mother in China. By 1865, they have prospered, but a fire in their store kills Lim's father and leaves Lim with nothing. Now homeless, Lim goes to Sacramento, where the first tracks of the Transcontinental Railroad are being laid. Joining the crew, he works hard not only for himself but also to buy the freedom of a Chinese slave girl.

ELSIE REIF ZIEGLER (1910–)
The Blowing-Wand (1955; 212 PAGES; M/M)

Today, everyone takes for granted the existence of glass in all of its forms. However, before the coming of machinery to produce glass, the art of glassblowing was a 4,000-year-old art. Glassblowers handed down their secrets from generation to generation, and the art moved from one European country of dominance to another. In the eighteenth century, Bohemia—then an independent kingdom—was the dominant glass-blowing country. Immigrants eventually brought their skills to America and mid-nineteenth-century Ohio, the setting of this story. Jaroslav Piontek, the hero, becomes an apprentice. He competes with other glass-makers, fighting to keep the secrets of his craft in a period when many craftsmen of the day are about to be swept away by the coming of industry.

NORMAN ZOLLINGER (1921–)
Riders to Cibola (1977; 258 PAGES; M/M)

New Mexico, in its last years as a territory, is the scene for a story that spans the first half of the twentieth century. Ten-year-old Ignacio Ortez is an orphaned Mexican boy who lives at a mission. Dissatisfied, he runs away and eventually becomes a rider at the Douglas MacAndrew cattle ranch. Caught between two cultures—his own and the still-developing white American one—Ignacio works at becoming an American cowboy. He and three generations of the MacAndrew family participate in events that range from Mexican revolutionary Pancho Villa's activities on the border, through two World Wars, to the flash of the first atomic bomb at Los Alamos, indicating the start of the nuclear war age.

Arrangement II:

Chronology

I. A Land of Promise (Pre-Encounter–1600)

Betty Baker. *Walk the World's Rim*
Sonia Levitin. *Roanoke: A Novel of the Lost Colony*
Joyce Rockwood. *Long Man's Song*
———. *To Spoil the Sun*
Mary Q. Steele and William O. Steele. *The Eye in the Forest*
William O. Steele. *The Wilderness Tattoo*

II. Building the Colonies (1600–1763)

Avi. *Encounter at Easton*
Patricia Clapp. *Constance: A Story of Early Plymouth*
Elizabeth Coatsworth. *Sword of the Wilderness*
James Fenimore Cooper. *The Deerslayer*
———. *The Last of the Mohicans*
———. *The Pathfinder*
Anne Eliot Crompton. *The Ice Trail*
Walter D. Edmonds. *The Matchlock Gun*
Norma Farber. *Mercy Short*
Rachel Field. *Calico Bush*
Leonard Everett Fisher. *The Warlock of Westfall*
Nathaniel Hawthorne. *The Scarlet Letter*
Jackie French Koller. *The Primrose Way*
Jean Lee Latham. *This Dear-Bought Land*
Lois Lenski. *Indian Captive: A Story of Mary Jemison*
Enid LaMonte Meadowcraft. *The First Year*
Ann Petry. *Tituba of Salem Village*
Kenneth Roberts. *Northwest Passage*
Elizabeth George Speare. *Calico Captive*
———. *The Prospering*
———. *The Witch of Blackbird Pond*
William O. Steele. *Flaming Arrows*
———. *Trail Through Danger*
Manly Wade Wellman. *Jamestown Adventure*

III. Winning Independence (1763–1789)

Harriette Arnow. *The Kentucky Trace*
Avi. *The Fighting Ground*
Shirley Barker. *The Road to Bunker Hill*
John and Patricia Beatty. *Who Comes to King's Mountain?*
Lorna Beers. *The Crystal Cornerstone*
Kensil Bell. *Jersey Rebel*
John Brick. *Captives of the Senecas*
Patricia Clapp. *I'm Deborah Sampson*
James Lincoln Collier and Christopher Collier. *Jump Ship to Freedom*

————. *My Brother Sam Is Dead*
————. *The Winter Hero*
Walter D. Edmonds. *Drums Along the Mohawk*
Sally Edwards. *George Midgett's War*
Howard Fast. *April Morning*
Ann Finlayson. *Greenhorn on the Frontier*
————. *Rebecca's War*
Inglis Fletcher. *The Wind in the Forest*
Esther Forbes. *Johnny Tremain*
Jean Fritz. *The Cabin Faced West*
————. *Early Thunder*
Janice Holt Giles. *The Kentuckians*
Wilma Pitchford Hays. *The Scarlet Badge*
Janet Hickman. *The Valley of the Shadow*
Nora Benjamin Kubie. *Joel*
Jean Lee Latham. *Carry On, Mr. Bowditch*
Isabelle Lawrence. *Drumbeats in Williamsburg*
James A. Michener. *Legacy**
Scott O'Dell. *Sarah Bishop*
Conrad Richter. *A Country of Strangers*
————. *The Light in the Forest*
Ann Rinaldi. *A Ride into Morning*
Richard F. Snow. *Freelon Starbird*
Elizabeth George Speare. *The Sign of the Beaver*
Robert M. Spector. *Salt Water Guns*
William O. Steele. *The Man with the Silver Eyes*
————. *Winter Danger*
————. *The Year of the Bloody Sevens*
Irving Stone. *Those Who Love*
Manly Wade Wellman. *Battle for King's Mountain*
————. *The South Fork Rangers*
Leonard Wibberley. *John Treegate's Musket*
————. *Peter Treegate's War*
————. *Sea Captain from Salem*
————. *Treegate's Raiders*

IV. Building the Nation (1789–1860)

Nathaniel Benchley. *Portrait of a Scoundrel*
Joan W. Blos. *A Gathering of Days*
Barbara Chase-Riboud. *Sally Hemings*
K. Follis Cheatham. *Bring Home the Ghost*
Elizabeth Coatsworth. *Here I Stay*
James Lincoln Collier and Christopher Collier. *The Clock*
James Fenimore Cooper. *The Pioneers*

---

*An asterisk denotes a novel that crosses several time periods.

———. *The Prairie*
Betty Sue Cummings. *Now, Ameriky*
Cynthia DeFelice. *Weasel*
John D. Fitzgerald. *Brave Buffalo Fighter*
Ed Foster. *Tejanos*
James R. French. *Nauvoo*
Jean Fritz. *Brady*
Lynne Gessner. *Navajo Slave*
Arnold A. Griese. *The Way of Our People*
Alex Haley. *A Different Kind of Christmas*
Walter and Marion Havighurst. *Song of the Pines*
Nathaniel Hawthorne. *The House of the Seven Gables*
Marcy Heidish. *Miracles*
Cecelia Holland. *The Bear Flag*
Elizabeth Howard. *The Courage of Bethea*
———. *Out of Step with the Dancers*
Evan Hunter. *The Chisholms*
Donald Jackson. *Valley Men*
Wayman Jones. *Edge of Two Worlds*
Jan Jordan. *Give Me the Wind*
Evelyn Sibley Lampman. *Cayuse Courage*
———. *Tree Wagon*
———. *Wheels West*
Rose Wilder Lane. *Young Pioneers*
Kathryn Lasky. *Beyond the Divide*
Athena V. Lord. *A Spirit to Ride the Whirlwind*
Robert M. McClung. *Hugh Glass, Mountain Man*
Eloise Jarvic McGraw. *Moccasin Trail*
Stephen W. Meader. *Boy with a Pack*
———. *Keep 'em Rolling*
Enid LaMonte Meadowcraft. *By Wagon and Flatboat*
———. *We Were There at the Opening of the Erie Canal*
Louise Moeri. *Save Queen of Sheba*
Liza Ketchum Murrow. *West Against the Wind*
Scott O'Dell. *Carlota*
———. *Island of the Blue Dolphins*
———. *Streams to the River, River to the Sea*
Katherine Paterson. *Lyddie*
Conrad Richter. *The Fields*
———. *The Town*
———. *The Trees*
Ann Rinaldi. *Wolf by the Ears*
Rose Sobol. *Woman Chief*
William O. Steele. *The Lone Hunt*
Irving Stone. *The President's Lady*
William Styron. *The Confessions of Nat Turner*
Mark Twain. *Adventures of Huckleberry Finn*

————. *Tom Sawyer*
Betty Underwood. *The Tamarack Tree*
Gore Vidal. *Burr*
Willard M. Wallace. *Jonathan Dearborn*
Luke Wallin. *In the Shadow of the Wind*
Jessamyn West. *Except for Me and Thee*
————. *The Friendly Persuasion*
————. *The Massacre at Fall Creek*
Leonard Wibberley. *The Last Battle*
————. *Leopard's Prey*
————. *Red Pawns*
Jane Yolen. *The Gift of Sarah Barker*
Blaine M. Yorgason. *Massacre at Salt Creek*
Elsie Reif Ziegler. *The Blowing-Wand*

V. The Nation Divides and Reunites
(1850's–1870's)

Judith MacBain Alter. *Luke and the Van Zandt County War*
Don Bannister. *Long Day at Shiloh*
Patricia Beatty. *Be Ever Hopeful, Hannalee*
————. *Charley Skedaddle*
————. *Jayhawker*
————. *Wait for Me, Watch for Me, Eula Bee*
Peter Burchard. *North by Night*
Stephen Crane. *The Red Badge of Courage*
Howard Fast. *Freedom Road*
Paul Fleischman. *Bull Run*
Jesse Hill Ford. *The Raider*
Patricia Lee Gauch. *Thunder at Gettysburg*
Betsy Haynes. *Cowslip*
Janet Hickman. *Zoar Blue*
Irene Hunt. *Across Five Aprils*
Douglas C. Jones. *Elkhorn Tavern*
MacKinlay Kantor. *Andersonville*
Harold Keith. *Rifles for Watie*
Thomas Keneally. *Confederates*
William Kennedy. *Quinn's Book*
Mary E. Lyons. *Letters from a Slave Girl: The Story of Harriet Jacobs* *
F. VanWyck Mason. *Armored Giants*
————. *Trumpets Sound No More*
Enid LaMonte Meadowcraft. *By Secret Railway*
Margaret Mitchell. *Gone with the Wind*
André Norton. *Ride Proud, Rebel!*
Scott O'Dell. *Sing Down the Moon*
Ann Rinaldi. *In My Father's House*

———. *The Last Silk Dress*
Michael Shaara. *The Killer Angels*
Barbara Smucker. *Runaway to Freedom: A Story of the Underground Railway*
William O. Steele. *The Perilous Road*
Robert J. Steelman. *The Galvanized Reb*
Irving Stone. *Love Is Eternal*
Harriet Beecher Stowe. *Uncle Tom's Cabin*
Margaret Walker. *Jubilee*
Tom Wicker. *Unto This Hour*

VI. A Time of Transformation: Settlement and Closing of the Western Frontier (1860's–1917)

Patricia Beatty. *Eight Mules from Monterey*
———. *Hail Columbia*
———. *How Many Miles to Sundown*
———. *Just Some Weeds from the Wilderness*
———. *Something to Shout About*
———. *That's One Ornery Orphan*
Nathaniel Benchley. *Only Earth and Sky Last Forever*
Hal Borland. *When the Legends Die*
Carol Ryrie Brink. *Caddie Woodlawn*
Dee Brown. *Killdeer Mountain*
Willa Cather. *My Ántonia*
———. *O Pioneers!*
Ann Nolan Clark. *All This Wild Land*
Howard Fast. *The Immigrants**
Edna Ferber. *Cimarron*
Edna Ferber. *So Big**
Elsie Kimmell Field. *Prairie Winter*
James Forman. *The Life and Death of Yellow Bird*
Kristiana Gregory. *Jenny of the Tetons*
Jamake Highwater. *Eyes of Darkness*
Douglas C. Jones. *The Court-Martial of George Armstrong Custer*
———. *A Creek Called Wounded Knee*
———. *Gone the Dreams and Dancing*
Harold Keith. *Komantcia*
Ruthanne Lum McCunn. *Thousand Pieces of Gold**
Charles K. Mills. *A Mighty Afternoon*
Scott O'Dell. *Zia*
Scott O'Dell and Elizabeth Hall. *Thunder Rolling in the Mountains*
Anne Pellowski. *First Farm in the Valley: Anna's Story*
———. *Stairstep Farm: Anna Rose's Story*
———. *Willow Wind Farm: Betsy's Story*
———. *Winding Valley Farm: Annie's Story*
Conrad Richter. *The Sea of Grass*

Virginia Driving Hawk Sneve. *Betrayed*
Charlene Jay Talbot. *An Orphan for Nebraska*
Ann Turner. *Grasshopper Summer*
Yoshiko Uchida. *Samurai of Gold Hill*
Dale Van Every. *The Day the Sun Died*
Owen Wister. *The Virginian*
Richard Wormser. *The Black Mustanger*
Alida E. Young. *Land of the Iron Dragon*
Norman Zollinger. *Riders to Cibola**

VII. A Time of Transformation: Industrialization, Urbanization, Modernization (1860's–1920's)

Sherwood Anderson. *Poor White*
Helen Tann Aschmann. *Connie Bell, M.D.*
Ted Birkman. *To Seize the Passing Dream**
Carole Bolton. *Never Jam Today*
Taylor Caldwell. *Captains and the Kings**
Kate Chopin. *The Awakening*
Edna Ferber. *Great Son**
———. *Show Boat*
Jane Flory. *The Liberation of Clementine Tipton*
Kristiana Gregory. *Earthquake at Dawn*
William Dean Howells. *The Rise of Silas Lapham*
Irene Hunt. *Claws of a Young Century*
Joan King. *Impressionist**
Sinclair Lewis. *Elmer Gantry*
John P. Marquand. *The Late George Apley**
Henry Roth. *Call It Sleep*
Marilyn Sacks. *Call Me Ruth*
Ouida Sebestyen. *Words by Heart*
Eileen Bluestone Sherman. *Independence Avenue*
Robert Skimin. *Chikara!**
Gloria Skurzynski. *The Tempering*
Upton Sinclair. *The Jungle*
Irving Stone. *Adversary in the House*
———. *Immortal Wife**
Booth Tarkington. *The Magnificent Ambersons*
Gore Vidal. *1876*
———. *Empire*
Edith Wharton. *The House of Mirth*
Laurence Yep. *The Star Fisher*

VIII. World War I and the 1920's

Willa Cather. *One of Ours*
John Dos Passos. *Three Soldiers*
Theodore Dreiser. *An American Tragedy*
Edna Ferber. *Giant**
F. Scott Fitzgerald. *The Great Gatsby*
Sinclair Lewis. *Arrowsmith**
———. *Babbitt*
———. *Main Street*
Robert Newton Peck. *Arly*
Upton Sinclair. *The Flivver King**
———. *World's End*
Gloria Skurzynski. *Good-bye, Billy Radish*

IX. The Great Depression and the New Deal (1920's–1940's)

Forrest Carter. *The Education of Little Tree*
Hila Colman. *Ellie's Inheritance*
Ralph Ellison. *Invisible Man**
James T. Farrell. *Studs Lonigan: A Trilogy**
Doris Gates. *Blue Willow*
J.M. Hayes. *The Grey Pilgrim*
William H. Hooks. *Circle of Fire*
———. *Crossing the Line*
Irene Hunt. *No Promises in the Wind*
Jackie French Koller. *Nothing to Fear*
Harper Lee. *To Kill a Mockingbird*
Wright Morris. *Plains Song: For Female Voices**
Michele Murray. *The Crystal Nights*
Phyllis Reynolds Naylor. *Walking Through the Dark*
Adrienne Richard. *Pistol*
John Steinbeck. *The Grapes of Wrath*
Mildred D. Taylor. *The Friendship*
———. *Let the Circle Be Unbroken*
———. *Mississippi Bridge*
———. *Roll of Thunder, Hear My Cry*
Crystal Thrasher. *Between Dark and Daylight*
———. *The Dark Didn't Catch Me*
———. *End of a Dark Road*
———. *A Taste of Daylight*
Alice Walker. *The Color Purple**
Robert Penn Warren. *All the King's Men*
Richard Wright. *Native Son*

X. World War II at Home and Abroad
(1939–1945)

Harriette Arnow. *The Dollmaker* *
Edward Beach. *Run Silent, Run Deep*
Larry Bograd. *Los Alamos Light*
Frank Bonham. *The Ghost Front*
———. *War Beneath the Sea*
Robert Burch. *Hut School and the Wartime Home-Front Heroes*
Howard Fast. *Second Generation* *
Connnie Jordan Green. *The War at Home*
Bette Greene. *Summer of My German Soldier*
Joseph Heller. *Catch-22*
John Hersey. *A Bell for Adano*
William P. McGivern. *Soldiers of '44*
Leo Rosten. *Captain Newman, M.D.*
William Saroyan. *The Human Comedy*
Doris Buchanan Smith. *Salted Lemons*
Yoshiko Uchida. *A Jar of Dreams*
———. *Journey Home*
———. *Journey to Topaz*
Robb White. *Flight Deck*
———. *Surrender*
———. *Torpedo Run*
———. *Up Periscope*
Herman Wouk. *War and Remembrance*
———. *The Winds of War*

XI. The Cold War and American Politics
(1940's–1970's)

Eugene Burdick and Harvey Wheeler. *Fail-Safe*
W.E. Butterworth. *Orders to Vietnam*
Allen Drury. *Advise and Consent*
———. *Capable of Honor*
———. *Preserve and Protect*
———. *A Shade of Difference*
Eloise Engle. *Dawn Mission: A Flight Nurse in Korea*
Howard Fast. *The Outsider*
Winston Groom. *Better Times Than These*
James Hickey. *Chrysanthemum in the Snow*
Laura Z. Hobson. *Gentleman's Agreement*
Annabel and Edgar Johnson. *The Last Knife*
Fletcher Knebel and Charles W. Bailey II. *Seven Days in May*
William J. Lederer and Eugene Burdick. *Sarkhan*
———. *The Ugly American*

Walter Dean Myers. *Fallen Angels*
Jayne Pettit. *My Name Is San Ho*
Edwin O'Connor. *The Last Hurrah*
Gore Vidal. *Washington, D.C.*
Morris L. West. *The Ambassador*
John A. Williams. *Captain Blackman**

XII. The Civil Rights Era and America Today (1950's–1980's)

Patricia Beatty. *Lupita Mañana*
Bebe Moore Campbell. *Your Blues Ain't Like Mine*
Natalie Savage Carlson. *The Empty Schoolhouse*
———. *Marchers for the Dream*
Edna Walker Chandler. *Indian Paintbrush*
Mary Downing Hahn. *December Stillness*
Yvette Moore. *Freedom Songs*
Dorothy Sterling. *Mary Jane*
Alice Walker. *Meridian*

XIII. Possible Futures

Margaret Atwood. *The Handmaid's Tale*
Nancy Bond. *The Voyage Begun*
John Hersey. *The Child Buyer*
Louise Moeri. *Downwind*
Robert C. O'Brien. *Z for Zachariah*

❖

ARRANGEMENT III:

THEMES

❖

I. Colonial Life and the Pioneer

(These novels take place in areas east of the Ohio and Mississippi rivers
from the late 1500's to the Revolutionary War period.)

Avi. *Encounter at Easton*
Patricia Clapp. *Constance: A Story of Early Plymouth*
Elizabeth Coatsworth. *Here I Stay*
————. *Sword of the Wilderness*
James Fenimore Cooper. *The Deerslayer*
————. *The Pathfinder*
————. *The Pioneers*
Walter D. Edmonds. *The Matchlock Gun*
Rachel Field. *Calico Bush*
Ann Finlayson. *Greenhorn on the Frontier*
Leonard Everett Fisher. *The Warlock of Westfall*
Inglis Fletcher. *The Wind in the Forest*
Jean Fritz. *The Cabin Faced West*
Jean Lee Latham. *This Dear-Bought Land*
Sonia Levitin. *Roanoke: A Novel of the Lost Colony*
Enid LaMonte Meadowcraft. *The First Year*
Elizabeth George Speare. *Calico Captive*
————. *The Prospering*
————. *The Sign of the Beaver*
————. *The Witch of Blackbird Pond*
William O. Steele. *Trail Through Danger*
————. *Winter Danger*
Manly Wade Wellman. *Jamestown Adventure*

II. The Spirit of the Western Frontier and the Pioneer

(These novels take place in Kentucky and areas west of the
Ohio and Mississippi rivers from the late 1700's to the early 1900's.)

Patricia Beatty. *Eight Mules from Monterey*
————. *How Many Miles to Sundown*
Carol Ryrie Brink. *Caddie Woodlawn*
Willa Cather. *My Ántonia*
————. *O Pioneers!*
James Fenimore Cooper. *The Prairie*
Edna Ferber. *Cimarron*
Elsie Kimmell Field. *Prairie Winter*
John D. Fitzgerald. *Brave Buffalo Fighter*
Ed Foster. *Tejanos*
Janice Holt Giles. *The Kentuckians*
Cecelia Holland. *The Bear Flag*

Evan Hunter. *The Chisholms*
Evelyn Sibley Lampman. *Tree Wagon*
————. *Wheels West*
Rose Wilder Lane. *Young Pioneers*
Kathryn Lasky. *Beyond the Divide*
Stephen W. Meader. *Keep 'em Rolling*
Liza Ketchum Murrow. *West Against the Wind*
Conrad Richter. *The Fields*
————. *The Sea of Grass*
————. *The Town*
————. *The Trees*
Ann Turner. *Grasshopper Summer*
Owen Wister. *The Virginian*

III. The Native-American Experience in America

(all periods)

Nathaniel Benchley. *Only Earth and Sky Last Forever*
John Brick. *Captives of the Senecas*
Forrest Carter. *The Education of Little Tree*
James Fenimore Cooper. *The Last of the Mohicans*
Anne Eliot Crompton. *The Ice Trail*
James Forman. *The Life and Death of Yellow Bird*
Lynne Gessner. *Navajo Slave*
Kristiana Gregory. *Jenny of the Tetons*
J.M. Hayes. *The Grey Pilgrim*
Jamake Highwater. *Eyes of Darkness*
Douglas C. Jones. *A Creek Called Wounded Knee*
————. *Gone the Dreams and Dancing*
Weyman Jones. *Edge of Two Worlds*
Jan Jordan. *Give Me the Wind*
Jackie French Koller. *The Primrose Way*
Evelyn Sibley Lampman. *Cayuse Courage*
Lois Lenski. *Indian Captive: A Story of Mary Jemison*
Charles K. Mills. *A Mighty Afternoon*
Scott O'Dell. *Sing Down the Moon*
————. *Zia*
Joyce Rockwood. *To Spoil the Sun*
Virginia Driving Hawk Sneve. *Betrayed*
Rose Sobol. *Woman Chief*
Elizabeth George Speare. *The Prospering*
Mary Q. Steele and William O. Steele. *The Eye in the Forest*
William O. Steele. *The Man with the Silver Eyes*
Dale Van Every. *The Day the Sun Died*
Luke Wallin. *In the Shadow of the Wind*

IV. The Revolutionary War Era

Harriette Arnow. *The Kentucky Trace*
Avi. *The Fighting Ground*
Shirley Barker. *The Road to Bunker Hill*
John and Patricia Beatty. *Who Comes to King's Mountain?*
Lorna Beers. *The Crystal Cornerstone*
Kensil Bell. *Jersey Rebel*
James Lincoln Collier and Christopher Collier. *My Brother Sam Is Dead*
Walter D. Edmonds. *Drums Along the Mohawk*
Sally Edwards. *George Midgett's War*
Howard Fast. *April Morning*
Esther Forbes. *Johnny Tremain*
Jean Fritz. *Early Thunder*
Wilma Pitchford Hays. *The Scarlet Badge*
Janet Hickman. *The Valley of the Shadow*
Isabelle Lawrence. *Drumbeats in Williamsburg*
Richard F. Snow. *Freelon Starbird*
Robert M. Spector. *Salt Water Guns*
William O. Steele. *The Year of the Bloody Sevens*
Manly Wade Wellman. *Battle for King's Mountain*
————. *The South Fork Rangers*
Leonard Wibberley. *John Treegate's Musket*
————. *Peter Treegate's War*
————. *Sea Captain from Salem*
————. *Treegate's Raiders*

V. The Civil War Era

Don Bannister. *Long Day at Shiloh*
Patricia Beatty. *Jayhawker*
Peter Burchard. *North by Night*
Stephen Crane. *The Red Badge of Courage*
Paul Fleischman. *Bull Run*
Jesse Hill Ford. *The Raider*
Patricia Lee Gauch. *Thunder at Gettysburg*
Irene Hunt. *Across Five Aprils*
Douglas C. Jones. *Elkhorn Tavern*
MacKinlay Kantor. *Andersonville*
Harold Keith. *Rifles for Watie*
Thomas Keneally. *Confederates*
F. Van Wyck Mason. *Armored Giants*
————. *Trumpets Sound No More*
Margaret Mitchell. *Gone with the Wind*
André Norton. *Ride Proud, Rebel!*
Ann Rinaldi. *In My Father's House*
————. *The Last Silk Dress*
Michael Shaara. *The Killer Angels*

William O. Steele. *The Perilous Road*
Robert J. Steelman. *The Galvanized Reb*
Tom Wicker. *Unto This Hour*

VI. The African-American Experience in America

(all periods)

Bebe Moore Campbell. *Your Blues Ain't Like Mine*
Natalie Savage Carlson. *The Empty Schoolhouse*
———. *Marchers for the Dream*
Barbara Chase-Riboud. *Sally Hemings*
K. Follis Cheatham. *Bring Home the Ghost*
James Lincoln Collier. *Jump Ship to Freedom*
Allen Drury. *A Shade of Difference*
Ralph Ellison. *Invisible Man*
Howard Fast. *Freedom Road*
Alex Haley. *A Different Kind of Christmas*
Betsy Haynes. *Cowslip*
William H. Hooks. *Circle of Fire*
———. *Crossing the Line*
Harper Lee. *To Kill a Mockingbird*
Mary E. Lyons. *Letters from a Slave Girl: The Story of Harriet Jacobs*
Enid LaMonte Meadowcraft. *By Secret Railway*
Ann Petry. *Tituba of Salem Village*
Ouida Sebestyen. *Words by Heart*
Barbara Smucker. *Runaway to Freedom*
Dorothy Sterling. *Mary Jane*
Harriet Beecher Stowe. *Uncle Tom's Cabin*
William Styron. *The Confessions of Nat Turner*
Mildred D. Taylor. *The Friendship*
———. *Let the Circle Be Unbroken*
———. *Mississippi Bridge*
———. *Roll of Thunder, Hear My Cry*
Alice Walker. *Meridian*
Margaret Walker. *Jubilee*
John A. Williams. *Captain Blackman*
Richard Wormser. *The Black Mustanger*
Richard Wright. *Native Son*

VII. Women in American Life

(all periods)

Helen Tann Aschmann. *Connie Bell, M.D.*
Margaret Atwood. *The Handmaid's Tale*
Patricia Beatty. *Hail Columbia*
———. *Just Some Weeds from the Wilderness*
Carole Bolton. *Never Jam Today*
Willa Cather. *My Ántonia*
———. *O Pioneers!*
Barbara Chase-Riboud. *Sally Hemings*
Kate Chopin. *The Awakening*
Patricia Clapp. *Constance*
———. *I'm Deborah Sampson*
Elizabeth Coatsworth. *Here I Stay*
Eloise Engle. *Dawn Mission: A Flight Nurse in Korea*
Norma Farber. *Mercy Short*
Edna Ferber. *Show Boat*
———. *So Big*
Ann Finlayson. *Rebecca's War*
Jane Flory. *The Liberation of Clementine Tipton*
Kristiana Gregory. *Jenny of the Tetons*
Marcy Heidish. *Miracles*
Elizabeth Howard. *The Courage of Bethea*
Irene Hunt. *Claws of a Young Century*
Joan King. *Impressionist*
Evelyn Sibley Lampman. *Wheels West*
Athena V. Lord. *A Spirit to Ride the Whirlwind*
Mary E. Lyons. *Letters from a Slave Girl*
Ruthanne Lum McCunn. *Thousand Pieces of Gold*
Margaret Mitchell. *Gone with the Wind*
Wright Morris. *Plains Song: For Female Voices*
Scott O'Dell. *Carlota*
———. *Sarah Bishop*
———. *Streams to the River, River to the Sea*
Katherine Paterson. *Lyddie*
Ann Petry. *Tituba of Salem Village*
Rose Sobol. *Woman Chief*
Elizabeth George Speare. *The Witch of Blackbird Pond*
Irving Stone. *Immortal Wife*
———. *Love Is Eternal*
———. *Those Who Love*
Betty Underwood. *The Tamarack Tree*
Edith Wharton. *The House of Mirth*

VIII. The Immigrant Experience

Patricia Beatty. *Lupita Mañana* (Mexican)
Taylor Caldwell. *Captains and the Kings* (Irish)
Willa Cather. *One of Ours* (Scandinavian, Bohemian, German)
————. *O Pioneers!* (Norwegian)
E.W. Chandler. *Indian Paintbrush* (Mexican)
Ann Nolan Clark. *All This Wild Land* (Finnish)
Betty Sue Cummings. *Now, Ameriky* (Irish)
Howard Fast. *The Immigrants* (Multicultural; predominantly Italian)
————. *The Second Generation* (Multicultural)
Edna Ferber. *Giant* (Mexican)
Walter and Marion Havighurst. *Song of the Pines* (Norwegian)
Cecelia Holland. *The Bear Flag* (Mexican)
Nora Benjamin Kubie. *Joel* (Polish, Irish)
Ruthanne Lum McCunn. *Thousand Pieces of Gold* (Chinese)
Scott O'Dell. *Carlota* (Spanish)
————. *Zia* (Spanish)
Anne Pellowski. *First Farm in the Valley: Anna's Story* (Polish)
————. *Stairstep Farm: Anna Rose's Story* (Polish)
————. *Willow Wind Farm: Betsy's Story* (Polish)
————. *Winding Valley Farm: Annie's Story* (Polish)
Henry Roth. *Call It Sleep* (Polish, Jewish)
Marilyn Sacks. *Call Me Ruth* (Russian)
Eileen Bluestone Sherman. *Independence Avenue* (Russian, Jewish)
Robert Skimin. *Chikara!* (Japanese)
Yoshiko Uchida. *A Jar of Dreams* (Japanese)
————. *Journey Home* (Japanese)
————. *Journey to Topaz* (Japanese)
————. *Samurai of Gold Hill* (Japanese)
Laurence Yep. *The Star Fisher* (Chinese)
Alida E. Young. *Land of the Iron Dragon* (Chinese)
Elise Reif Ziegler. *The Blowing-Wand* (Bohemian)
Norman Zollinger. *Riders to Cibola* (Mexican)

IX. Politics; Political Commentary

Judith MacBain Alter. *Luke and the Van Zandt County War*
Eugene Burdick and Harvey Wheeler. *Fail-Safe*
Taylor Caldwell. *Captains and the Kings*
James Lincoln Collier and Christopher Collier. *The Winter Hero*
Allen Drury. *Advise and Consent*
————. *Capable of Honor*
————. *Preserve and Protect*
————. *A Shade of Difference*
Kristiana Gregory. *Earthquake at Dawn*
Annabel and Edgar Johnson. *The Last Knife*

William Kennedy. *Quinn's Book*
Fletcher Knebel and Charles W. Bailey, II. *Seven Days in May*
William J. Lederer and Eugene Burdick. *Sarkhan*
————. *The Ugly American*
James A. Michener. *Legacy*
Edwin O'Connor. *The Last Hurrah*
Upton Sinclair. *The Jungle*
Irving Stone. *Adversary in the House*
Gore Vidal. *Burr*
————. *1876*
————. *Empire*
————. *Washington, D.C.*
Robert Penn Warren. *All the King's Men*
Morris L. West. *The Ambassador*

X. Social Class; Social Criticism; Social Consciousness

Sherwood Anderson. *Poor White*
Patricia Beatty. *Be Ever Hopeful, Hannalee*
Edna Walker Chandler. *Indian Paintbrush*
James Lincoln Collier and Christopher Collier. *The Clock*
Hila Colman. *Ellie's Inheritance*
Howard Fast. *The Outsider*
Edna Ferber. *Giant*
————. *Show Boat*
F. Scott Fitzgerald. *The Great Gatsby*
Bette Greene. *Summer of My German Soldier*
Mary Downing Hahn. *December Stillness*
Nathaniel Hawthorne. *The House of the Seven Gables*
————. *The Scarlet Letter*
Doris Gates. *Blue Willow*
Laura Z. Hobson. *Gentleman's Agreement*
William Dean Howells. *The Rise of Silas Lapham*
Irene Hunt. *No Promises in the Wind*
Jackie French Koller. *Nothing to Fear*
Harper Lee. *To Kill a Mockingbird*
Sinclair Lewis. *Arrowsmith*
————. *Babbitt*
————. *Elmer Gantry*
————. *Main Street*
John P. Marquand. *The Late George Apley*
Michele Murray. *Crystal Nights*
Phyllis Reynolds Naylor. *Walking Through the Dark*
Robert Newton Peck. *Arly*
William Saroyan. *The Human Comedy*
Upton Sinclair. *The Flivver King*

———. *The Jungle*
Gloria Skurzynski. *The Tempering*
Doris Buchanan Smith. *Salted Lemons*
John Steinbeck. *The Grapes of Wrath*
Booth Tarkington. *The Magnificent Ambersons*
Crystal Thrasher. *Between Dark and Daylight*
———. *The Dark Didn't Catch Me*
———. *End of a Dark Road*
———. *A Taste of Daylight*
Mark Twain. *Adventures of Huckleberry Finn*
———. *Tom Sawyer*
Yoshiko Uchida. *A Jar of Dreams*
Jessamyn West. *Except for Me and Thee*

XI. Modern War in America (World War I, World War II, Korea, Vietnam)

Edward Beach. *Run Silent, Run Deep* (WWII)
Larry Bograd. *Los Alamos Light* (WWII)
Frank Bonham. *The Ghost Front* (WWII)
———. *War Beneath the Sea* (WWII)
Robert Burch. *Hut School and the Wartime Home-Front Heroes* (WWII)
W.E. Butterworth. *Orders to Vietnam* (Vietnam)
Willa Cather. *One of Ours* (WWI)
John Dos Passos. *Three Soldiers* (WWI)
Eloise Engle. *Dawn Mission: A Flight Nurse in Korea* (Korea)
Connie Jordan Green. *The War at Home* (WWII)
Bette Greene. *Summer of My German Soldier* (WWII)
Winston Groom. *Better Times Than These* (Vietnam)
Joseph Heller. *Catch-22* (WWII)
John Hersey. *A Bell for Adano* (WWII)
James Hickey. *Chrysanthemum in the Snow* (Korea)
Annabel and Edgar Johnson. *The Last Knife* (Vietnam)
William P. McGivern. *Soldiers of '44* (WWII)
Walter Dean Myers. *Fallen Angels* (Vietnam)
Jayne Pettit. *My Name Is San Ho* (Vietnam)
Leo Rosten. *Captain Newman, M.D.* (WWII)
Upton Sinclair. *World's End* (WWI)
Gloria Skurzynski. *Good-bye, Billy Radish* (WWI)
Morris L. West. *The Ambassador* (Vietnam)
Robb White. *Flight Deck* (WWII)
Robb White. *Surrender* (WWII)
———. *Torpedo Run* (WWII)
———. *Up Periscope* (WWII)
John A. Williams. *Captain Blackman* (all wars)
Herman Wouk. *War and Remembrance* (WWII)
———. *The Winds of War* (WWII)

ARRANGEMENT IV:

TITLES

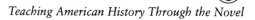

Supplemental Movie Listing

(An asterisk at the end of an entry indicates that the
movie is available on videocassette.)

HARRIETTE ARNOW

The Dollmaker (1984, 104 mins.) Jane Fonda, Levon Helm, Susan Kingsley, Nikki
  Cresswell. Made for television. Dir: Daniel Petrie.*

MARGARET ATWOOD

The Handmaid's Tale (1990, 118 mins.) Natasha Richardson, Faye Dunaway, Aidan
  Quinn, Elizabeth McGovern, Victoria Tennant, Robert Duvall, Blanche Baker, Traci
  Lind. Screenplay by Harold Pinter. Dir: Volker Schlondorff.*

CAPTAIN EDWARD BEACH

Run Silent, Run Deep (1958, 93 mins.) Clark Gable, Burt Lancaster, Don Rickles.
  Dir: Robert Wise.*

EUGENE BURDICK AND HARVEY WHEELER

Fail-Safe (1964, 111 mins.) Henry Fonda, Dan O'Herlihy, Walter Matthau. Dir: Sidney
  Lumet.*

JAMES FENIMORE COOPER

The Deerslayer (1957, 78 mins.) Lex Barker, Forrest Tucker, Rita Moreno. Dir: Kurt
  Neumann.
The Deerslayer (1978, 78 mins) Steve Forrest, Ned Romero. Made for television. Dir:
  Dick Friedenberg.*
The Last of the Mohicans (1936, 100 mins.) Randolph Scott, Binnie Barnes, Heather
  Angel. Dir: George B. Seitz.*
The Last of the Mohicans (1977, 104 mins.) Steve Forrest, Ned Romero, Andrew Prine,
  Don Shanks. Made for television. Dir: James L. Conway.*
The Last of the Mohicans (1992, 114 mins.) Daniel Day-Lewis, Madeleine Stowe, Jodhi
  May, Russell Means. Dir: Michael Mann.*
The Pathfinder (1952, 78 mins.) George Montgomery, Helena Carter, Jay Silverheels,
  Walter Kingsford, Elena Verdugo. Dir: Sidney Salkow.

STEPHEN CRANE

The Red Badge of Courage (1951, 69 mins.) Audie Murphy, Bill Mauldin, Arthur
  Hunnicutt, John Dierkes, Royal Dano, Andy Devine. Dir: John Huston.*
The Red Badge of Courage (1974, 74 mins.) Richard Thomas, Warren Berlinger, Wendell
  Burton, Charles Aidman. Made for television. Dir: Lee Philips.

THEODORE DREISER

An American Tragedy (1931, 95 mins.) Phillips Holmes, Sylvia Sidney, Frances Dee. Dir:
  Josef von Sternberg.

ALLEN DRURY

Advise and Consent (1962, 139 mins.) Henry Fonda, Walter Pidgeon, Charles Laughton,
  Don Murray, Lew Ayres, Gene Tierney, Franchot Tone, Burgess Meredith. Dir: Otto
  Preminger.*

WALTER D. EDMONDS

Drums Along the Mohawk (1939, 103 mins.) Claudette Colbert, Henry Fonda, Edna May Oliver. Dir: John Ford.*

JAMES T. FARRELL

Studs Lonigan (1960, 103 mins.) Christopher Knight, Frank Gorshin, Venetia Stevenson, Jack Nicholson. Dir: Irving Lerner.*

HOWARD FAST

April Morning (1988, 96 mins.) Tommy Lee Jones, Robert Urich, Chad Lowe, Susan Blakely, Meredith Salenger, Rip Torn. Made for television. Dir: Delbert Mann.

Freedom Road (1979, 208 mins.) Muhammad Ali, Kris Kristofferson, Ron O'Neal. Made for television. Dir: Jan Kadar.*

The Immigrants (1978, 200 mins.) Stephen Macht, Sharon Gless, Aimee Eccles, Richard Anderson, Susan Strasberg, Pernell Roberts, John Saxon. Made for television. Dir: Alan J. Levi.

EDNA FERBER

Cimarron (1931, 130 mins.) Richard Dix, Irene Dunne, Estelle Taylor. Dir: Wesley Ruggles.*

Cimarron (1960, 140 mins.) Glenn Ford, Maria Schell, Anne Baxter, Arthur O'Connell. Dir: Anthony Mann.

Giant (1956, 201 mins.) James Dean, Rock Hudson, Elizabeth Taylor, Carroll Baker, Dennis Hopper, Mercedes McCambridge, Chill Wills, Jane Withers, Sal Mineo, Earl Holliman, Rodney Taylor. Dir: George Stevens.*

Show Boat (1929, 130 mins.) Laura LaPlante, Alma Rubens, Elsie Barlett, Joseph Schild-kraut. Silent film with musical score added. Dir: Harry Pollard.

Show Boat (1936, 113 mins.) Irene Dunne, Allan Jones, Helen Morgan, Paul Robeson, Charles Winninger, Hattie McDaniel. Dir: James Whale.*

Show Boat (1951, 107 mins.) Kathryn Grayson, Howard Keel, Ava Gardner, Marge and Gower Champion, Joe E. Brown, Agnes Moorehead. Dir: George Sidney.*

So Big (1932, 90 mins.) Barbara Stanwyck, George Brent, Dickie Moore, Bette Davis, Guy Kibbee, Alan Hale. Dir: William A. Wellman.

So Big (1953, 101 mins.) Jane Wyman, Sterling Hayden. Dir: Robert Wise.

F. SCOTT FITZGERALD

The Great Gatsby (1949, 92 mins.) Alan Ladd, Betty Field, Barry Sullivan, Ruth Hussey, Macdonald Carey, Shelley Winters, Howard Da Silva. Dir: Elliott Nugent.

The Great Gatsby (1974, 144 mins.) Robert Redford, Mia Farrow, Karen Black, Sam Waterston, Bruce Dern, Scott Wilson, Howard Da Silva, Edward Herrmann, Patsy Kensit. Dir: Jack Clayton.*

ESTHER FORBES

Johnny Tremain (1957, 80 mins.) Hal Stalmaster, Juana Patten, Sebastian Cabot. Dir: Robert Stevenson.

BETTE GREENE

The Summer of My German Soldier (MTV, 1978, 104 mins.) Kristy McNichol, Michael Constantine, Bruce Davison, Esther Rolle. Dir: Michael Tuchner.*

NATHANIEL HAWTHORNE

The House of Seven Gables (1940, 89 mins.) George Sanders, Margaret Lindsay, Vincent Price. Dir: Joe May.

The Scarlet Letter (1926, 80 mins.) Lillian Gish, Lars Hanson, Henry B. Walthall, Karl Dane. Dir: Victor Sjostrom.

The Scarlet Letter (1934, 70 mins.) Colleen Moore, Hardie Albright, Henry B. Walthall, William Farnum, Alan Hale, Cora Sue Collins. Dir: Robert G. Vignola.*

The Scarlet Letter (1973, 94 mins.) Senta Berger, Hans Christian Blech, Lou Castel. Dir: Wim Winders.*

JOSEPH HELLER

Catch-22 (1970, 120 mins.) Alan Arkin, Martin Balsam, Richard Benjamin, Arthur Garfunkel, Jack Gilford, Bob Newhart, Anthony Perkins, Jon Voight. Dir: Mike Nichols.*

JOHN HERSEY

A Bell for Adano (1945, 103 mins.) John Hodiak, William Bendix, Gene Tierney, Richard Conte, Glenn Lagan, Harry Morgan. Dir: Henry King.

LAURA Z. HOBSON

Gentleman's Agreement (1947, 118 mins.) Gregory Peck, Dorothy McGuire, John Garfield, Anne Revere, Celeste Holm. Dir: Elia Kazan.

MACKINLAY KANTOR

The Andersonville Trial (1970, 150 mins.) Martin Sheen, William Shatner, Buddy Ebsen, Richard Basehart, Cameron Mitchell. Dir: George C. Scott.*

FLETCHER KNEBEL AND CHARLES W. BAILEY II

Seven Days in May (1964, 118 mins.) Burt Lancaster, Kirk Douglas, Ava Gardner, Fredric March, Edmond O'Brien. Dir: John Frankenheimer.*

ROSE WILDER LANE

The Young Pioneers (1976, 98 mins.) Linda Purl, Roger Kern. Made for television. Dir: Michael O'Herlihy.

WILLIAM J. LEDERER AND EUGENE BURDICK

The Ugly American (1963, 120 mins.) Marlon Brando, Eiji Okada, Arthur Hill, Jocelyn Brando. Dir: George H. Englund.*

HARPER LEE

To Kill a Mockingbird (1962, 129 mins.) Gregory Peck, Mary Badham, Philip Alford, Brock Peters. Dir: Robert Mulligan.*

SINCLAIR LEWIS

Elmer Gantry (1960, 145 mins.) Burt Lancaster, Jean Simmons, Dean Jagger, Arthur Kennedy, Shirley Jones, Patti Page. Dir: Richard Brooks.*

Arrowsmith (1931, 108 mins.) Ronald Colman, Helen Hayes, Richard Bennett, Myrna Loy. Dir: John Ford.*

Babbitt (1934, 74 mins.) Guy Kibbee, Aline MacMahon, Claire Dodd. Dir: William Keighley.

JOHN P. MARQUAND

The Late George Apley (1947, 98 mins.) Ronald Colman, Peggy Cummins. Dir: Joseph L. Mankiewicz.

MARGARET MITCHELL

Gone with the Wind (1939, 219 mins.) Clark Gable, Vivien Leigh, Leslie Howard, Olivia de Havilland, Hattie McDaniel, Butterfly McQueen, Thomas Mitchell, Ona Munson, Ann Rutherford, Evelyn Keyes, George Reeves, Laura Hope Crews. Dir: Victor Fleming.*

EDWIN O'CONNOR

The Last Hurrah (1958, 121 mins.) Spencer Tracy, Jeffrey Hunter, Pat O'Brien, Dianne Foster, Basil Rathbone, John Carradine, Jane Darwell, Donald Crisp, James Gleason. Dir: John Ford.

The Last Hurrah (1977, 104 mins.) Carroll O'Connor, Dana Andrews, Burgess Meredith, Mariette Hartley, John Anderson. Made for television. Dir: Vincent Sherman.

SCOTT O'DELL

Island of the Blue Dolphins (1964, 93 mins.) Celia Kaye, Larry Domasin, George Kennedy. Dir: James B. Clark.*

CONRAD RICHTER

The Light in the Forest (1958, 93 mins.) Fess Parker, Joanne Dru, Carol Lynley. Dir: Herschel Daugherty.*

KENNETH ROBERTS

Northwest Passage (1939, 125 mins.) Spencer Tracy, Robert Young, Walter Brennan. Dir: King Vidor.*

LEO ROSTEN

Captain Newman, M.D. (1963, 126 mins.) Gregory Peck, Tony Curtis, Angie Dickinson, Eddie Albert, Bobby Darin. Dir: David Miller.*

WILLIAM SAROYAN

The Human Comedy (1943, 118 mins.) Mickey Rooney, Frank Morgan, Marsha Hunt, Van Johnson. Dir: Clarence Brown.*

JOHN STEINBECK

The Grapes of Wrath (1940, 128 mins.) Henry Fonda, Jane Darwell, John Carradine, Charley Grapewin, Dorris Bowden, John Qualen. Dir: John Ford.*

IRVING STONE

The President's Lady (1953, 96 mins.) Susan Hayward, Charlton Heston, Fay Bainter, Carl Betz, John McIntire. Dir: Henry Levin.

HARRIET BEECHER STOWE

Uncle Tom's Cabin (1965, 118 mins.) John Kitzmiller, Herbert Lom, O.W. Fisher, Eleonora Rossi-Drago, Eartha Kitt. Dir: Geza Radvanyi.*

Uncle Tom's Cabin (1987, 108 mins.) Avery Brooks, Phylicia Rashad, Edward Woodward, Bruce Dern, Frank Converse. Made for cable television. Dir: Stan Lathan.

BOOTH TARKINGTON

The Magnificent Ambersons (1942, 88 mins.) Joseph Cotten, Tim Holt, Anne Baxter, Dolores Costello, Ray Collins, Agnes Moorehead, Richard Bennett, Erskine Sanford. Dir: Orson Welles.*

MARK TWAIN

The Adventures of Huckleberry Finn (1939, 110 mins.) Mickey Rooney, William Frawley, Walter Connolly. Dir: Richard Thorpe.*

The Adventures of Huckleberry Finn (1960, 107 mins.) Tony Randall, Eddie Hodges, Judy Canova, Archie Moore, Andy Devine. Dir: Michael Curtiz.

The Adventures of Huckleberry Finn (1981, 104 mins.) Kurt Ida, Dan Monahan, Brock Peters, Forrest Tucker. Made for television. Dir: Jack Hively.*

Huckleberry Finn (1931, 80 mins.) Jackie Coogan, Mitzi Green, Junior Durkin, Eugene Pallette, Jackie Searl, Jane Darwell, Clarence Muse. Dir: Norman Taurog.

Huckleberry Finn (1939, 90 mins.) Mickey Rooney, Rex Ingram, Walter Connolly, William Frawley, Victor Kilian. Dir: Richard Thorpe.

Huckleberry Finn (1974, 113 mins.) Musical version. Paul Winfield, Harvey Korman, David Wayne, Jeff East. Dir: J. Lee Thompson.*

Huckleberry Finn (1975, 104 mins.) Ron Howard, Donny Most, Antonio Fargas, Jack Elam, Royal Dano, Merle Haggard. Made for television. Dir: Robert Totten.*

The Adventures of Tom Sawyer (1938, 93 mins.) Tommy Kelly, May Robson, Victor Jory. Dir: Norman Taurog.*

Tom Sawyer (1930, 86 mins.) Jackie Coogan, Mitzi Green, Junior Durkin. Dir: John Cromwell.

Tom Sawyer (1973, 104 mins.) Josh Albee, Jeff Tyler, Jane Wyatt, Buddy Ebsen, Vic Morrow, John McGiver. Made for television. Dir: James Neilson.

Tom Sawyer (1973, 104 mins.) Musical version. Johnny Whitaker, Celeste Holm, Warren Oates, Jeff East, Jodie Foster. Dir: Don Taylor.*

ALICE WALKER

The Color Purple (1985, 155 mins.) Whoopi Goldberg, Danny Glover, Rae Dawn Chong, Margaret Avery, Oprah Winfrey. Dir: Steven Spielberg.*

ROBERT PENN WARREN

All the King's Men (1949, 109 mins.) Broderick Crawford, Joanne Dru, John Ireland, Mercedes McCambridge, John Derek, Shepherd Strudwick, Anne Seymour. Dir: Robert Rossen.*

JESSAMYN WEST

Friendly Persuasion (1956, 139 mins.) Gary Cooper, Dorothy McGuire, Tony Perkins, Marjorie Main. Dir: William Wyler.*

Friendly Persuasion (1975, 104 mins.) Richard Kiley, Shirley Knight, Clifton James, Michael O'Keefe, Kevin O'Keefe. Made for television. Dir: Joseph Sargent.

OWEN WISTER

The Virginian (1929, 90 mins.) Gary Cooper, Richard Arlen, Walter Hudson, Mary Brian. Dir: Victor Fleming.*

HERMAN WOUK

The Winds of War (1983, 883 mins.) Robert Mitchum, Ali McGraw, Polly Bergen, Jan-Michael Vincent, John Houseman, Victoria Tennant, Peter Graves, Ralph Bellamy. Made for television. Dir: Dan Curtis.*

RICHARD WRIGHT

Native Son (1950, 91 mins.) Richard Wright, Jean Wallace, Gloria Madison, Nicholas Joy. Dir: Pierre Chenal.*

Native Son (1986, 112 mins.) Carroll Baker, Akosua Busia, Matt Dillon, Victor Love, John Karlen, Elizabeth McGovern, Geraldine Page, David Rasche, Lane Smith, Oprah Winfrey. Dir: Jerrold Freedman.*

Index of Historical Characters and Events